"My Walk Through the Valley"

A True Testimony of God's Mighty Blessings in the <u>extreme</u> in the Life of James Crosson

JAMES F. CROSSON
611 CHESTNUT ST.
IRWIN, PA 15642-3535

Copyright © January 2013
James F. Crosson

* * * * *

Books available from
James Crosson
611 Chestnut St
Irwin, PA 15642-3535
(724) 864-3087

TABLE OF CONTENTS

Chapter 1
Violence on Chartiers Avenue   1

Chapter 2
J.C. vs. the U.S.M.C.   23

Chapter 3
Good Morning, Viet Nam   31

Chapter 4
The Shot Heard Round the City   53

Chapter 5
"Getting Serious About God"   68

Chapter 6
Some Closing Thoughts   81

Never Ending Story Post Script   89

Dedications   91

Closing Thoughts   92

Chapter One
Violence on Chartiers Avenue

"The only thing my Dad ever gave me was a name. The only thing he left me was alone." – James F. Crosson

I should be dead right now! If that sounds unnecessarily melodramatic or depressing, let's take a detailed look at growing up under less than ideal circumstances.

I was born on June 3, 1947. Pittsburgh, Pennsylvania is my hometown. Soon after I made my wailing entrance into this already troubled world, my father walked out on my mother. No good-byes or fond farewells were to be had. He simply vanished ... a magician's grand performance.

The only thing my Dad ever gave me was a name. The only thing he left me was alone. My name, James Francis Crosson, proved useful for identification purposes; being alone proved far less useful. Granted, I wasn't alone literally. I had family around me but I was without a father figure. Not an outstanding way to begin a childhood.

So it was me, my mother, whose name was Beverly, and my two sisters, Candy and Carol. Candy is a year older than me. Carol is several years older. Carol did know my biological father but today gives him low marks because she remembers him as being verbally abusive to her. It will become obvious that my family tree, especially on the paternal side and with the later addition of a stepfather, was not the inspiration for the famous TV series "Father Knows Best"... unless we changed the title to "Father Was Crazy Enough to Think He Knew Best."

It took time for us to recover from my biological dad's unscheduled and unmistakably rude departure, but we did. Federal Street on the North side became my sandbox, though memories of those years are hazy. I tell people that I was born very young—most of my childhood was spent in my youth. If that sounds a bit absurd, remember that it was humor, perverse though it was, that got my family through many struggles.

My sister Carol reminded me that, after a brief stint on Federal Street, our earliest address was Reedsdale Street on the North Side. We lived on one of the higher floors of what was then considered "high-rise" apartments. I had many words to describe my living arrangements back then, but the one that would be least offensive to readers is "Dump in the Air", but it was the best we could afford, I guess.

The approximate spot where I once lived was recently occupied by Three Rivers Stadium. I lived immediately above what was Home Plate. Some people seem destined to hit home runs regardless of circumstances. As a headstrong young man growing up, I scored a disproportionate number of foul balls and strikeouts.

This was in contrast to the frame house on Chartiers Avenue where I spent most of my growing years. I remember my sister Carol having real potential as an artist. I was never sure about Candy's dreams. I always wanted to be a disc jockey. To me being a disc jockey was one of the most exciting jobs on earth. When my sister Candy dated a guy in the service, I used to give her poems, jokes and other neat junk for her to put in her letters to him. I think this was my vicarious way of being a disc jockey, awkward though it was. Had my life taken a different turn, I could have made it as a disc jockey, given my natural talents for music. Eventually, thanks to the introduction of a step dad to our family, survival took priority over dreams.

Mom had her hands full raising three kids in those circumstances. She was determined and tough as nails when she needed to be, but child rearing on a limited income took its toll. Mom had to put Candy and Carol in what was known back then as a boarding house. Being the baby, I stayed home.

Carol hated her new surroundings in an imposing looking building called Presley House. It was only a few miles from where we lived, but for Candy, and especially Carol, it was a universe away. Presley House was noble of mission and necessary to our needs. Candy and Carol never warmed up to it ...except on one occasion. Carol, in an interview with my collaborator for this work, Mike Pochan, described her "organized" attempt to burn down Presley House. When the appointed time came, the flames raged. Perhaps "raged" is too strong a word; how about flickered? Carol admits not taking into account the fact that Presley House was constructed of stone and concrete! The episode severely singed her relations with her keepers at Presley House, who revoked holiday privileges to visit home. When my mom remarried, Carol and Candy came home ...but only to discover another inferno in the making.

A new "knight in shining armor" had arrived on the scene. I'll call him Andy. This new father figure must have "sprung" my sisters from Presley House to bring them home. No one knew it at the time, but Andy's arrival on the scene represented "out of the frying pan and into the fire" for the lot of us. For a short time, it was the quiet before the storm. The man was emotionally disturbed and morally bankrupt.

Andy was a Navy man and proud of it. (Information leaked to me from various sources that Andy and the Navy got along as well as Andy and the rest of the world.) It would be futile to look for Andy's name teaching classes on winning friends and influencing people. But, I believe my mother was blinded by the need for male companionship. Financial stress, I'm sure, was also part of the decision. Otherwise, I can't imagine anyone with a clear head willingly picking Andy as a long-term partner.

No one could have known at the time, but two small incidents had a prophetic quality for my future life. The first occurred when my friends and I were playing in the apartment complex. The game was usually cops and robbers or cowboys and Indians played with reckless enthusiasm on the crisscrossing set of fire escapes. We were young. Safety? What was that? What could possibly happen? On that particular day I had been picked as a "bad guy". I had been "captured" and slated for "hanging". The situation was grim in our make believe scenario. (I didn't realize it at the time but the situation in real life was soon to be equally grim.) I was made by my "captors" to stand on a chair while a rope was strung over the top of one of the fire escapes above me. The chair was to be kicked out from under me and ... well ... scratch one villain. Only seconds before I would have knocked too early on the Pearly Gates, a neighbor lady saw a disaster and yanked me off the chair. My unexpected Savior promptly reprimanded me to my mother's care, who promptly gave me a resounding whack.

Another, even more noteworthy incident involved my run in with the neighborhood bully. The bully, already guilty of any number of transgressions against myself and my friends, had stolen one of my roller skates and was gloating over his ill-gotten gain. Impulsively, out of desperation and anger, I whacked the bully over the head with my remaining skate, laying open his skull and getting him a free trip to the hospital in an ambulance. In those days roller skates were made from tough metal and were quite capable of doing damage to human skin. I got in trouble from that little episode with everyone except my stepfather, who put his arm around my shoulder, said I had done a good thing and told me that was the way to handle such situations. That was the first and only time my stepfather gave me open encouragement. It would later serve as a powerful example of what not to expect. What kind of man congratulates his son for doing something that brutal?

I've discovered that before Andy arrived, my mother had a career. Carol told me that mom was a professional dancer. She was an exotic dancer in the days when sensuality had to be communicated while fully clothed in flesh colors or in a skimpy costume. Pictures I have seen of her portray a true beauty, one to be admired. I'm told that mom met Andy while she was dancing in a club. He was a bouncer. He should have bounced himself straight out of the picture!

Our next move as a family was to a frame house on Chartiers Avenue in Pittsburgh's West End. From day one, my stepfather and a certain headstrong youth were to be at odds. This constant conflict, along with my step dad's extensive attitude problems, was to set the pace for life on Chartiers Avenue. It would give us a storehouse of memories that should have been the exclusive province of cheap, sleazy fiction.

While in grade school, I came home with a spelling book. My stepfather would quiz me and, if I misspelled a word, he would hit me in the head, my head would bounce of his fist and then off the wall. It made me a nervous wreck. I would chew my fingernails to my elbows. Earlier on when I was little, I would be sitting there watching TV and he would punch me in the head and send me flying across the room. He would say that was for what he missed. I vowed that I would never treat my children like that and I never did.

I had no way of knowing what a real father was, much less how he should act. I came to assume that regular beatings were a normal part of the way a stepfather should behave. In short order, my stepfather created a new family unit. Now our family consisted of my sisters, eventually two stepbrothers, and me. I'll call them Andy Jr. and Bill. An optimist might say: "The more the merrier" and let it go at that. The situation that developed was anything but merry.

This "knight in shining armor" came with a dark hidden agenda. He had a moral corrosion unlike anything any of us had ever seen. None of us had any idea how much he would change our lives and nearly destroy us. We tried humor to put the best face on the situation, but nothing changed the reality of our lives under this new "father figure". His initial charm and warmth evaporated into a regime of physical, emotional, and mental abuse.

I was to discover rapidly that in Andy's world, no real provocation was needed to mete out punishment; any dark mood would do nicely. Add to the mix an active, rebellious kid and the situation was explosive. Oddly enough, I may inadvertently have provided the perfect complement to my stepfather's personality. I got into enough trouble to warrant discipline ... giving my stepfather a custom-made excuse to overreact and gloriously indulge his power fantasies.

While I didn't have much of a relationship with my sister Candy, Carol and I were close enough to cover each other's tracks. Carol lied to my stepfather more than once to save me from being beaten. Living in that house became an awkward course in survival training. My stepfather's dark side would systematically rob myself and my family of all self-esteem.

Once we were outside the confines of the house, we managed to let loose and have fun. Like "normal" kids, we had friends and did wild and crazy things. This helped to take our minds off the fact that the 'Gates of Hell' were never more than several blocks away.

In those days, for us being normal was being holy terrors. At this I was an expert! Usually "good kids" were discouraged or outright forbidden from hanging out with me, my brother, or my friends. At the time it didn't matter. Grade school pranksterism became one of my regrettable specialties. At the prompting of one of my friends I livened up a typing class my friend was in by replacing part of the typewriter ribbon with a string of caps!

Other low budget terrorism included sparks and flames. I added metal chair leg protectors to the bottom of my shoes and made the sparks fly when I stopped quickly on the marble floors in the school hallways. Many kids build paper airplanes; I had to go one better and build flaming paper airplanes sprinkled with lighter fluid. These burning paper airplanes were thrown in open office windows when we walked by them on our routes. It gave the office workers a great and instant excuse to get out of the office. In my defense, I don't recall any loss of life or extensive property damage but we ran too fast to really keep accurate records.

It's not that we didn't get involved in constructive projects. I remember one of our more ambitious endeavors was the construction of a sophisticated cabin. Some kids build tree houses; we built our very own sturdy cabin. It was not only sizable but also well constructed. We dragged full-size railroad ties from nearly a mile away! It was impregnable. One of my friends had a father who was in construction. This friend supplied the glue that literally sealed our cabin together. But, in all our work, sweat and toil, none of us noticed the bees' nest that literally rubbed against our cabin. When the time for conflict would come, these feisty insects had their own brand of retribution.

There was a second problem with our envied cabin. A disagreeable neighbor lived nearby. I can't say for sure, but we may have built our masterpiece on his property. Mr. Disagreeable Neighbor apparently made it his goal in life to remove our Home Sweet Home. Normal efforts on his part to do away with our cabin did not work. He decided to take more drastic action. One afternoon we arrived at our cabin to find one side blown out. The smell of gunpowder hung in the air. The suspect list was extremely short. It was time for action. That night, working from a plan orchestrated by Yours Truly, we circled Mr. Disagreeable Neighbor's house and, on cue, sent rocks shattering his windows. Every single one. We may been small, but we were mighty and we were mad.

Now, back to the bees. We managed to disrupt the hive thanks to a flaming arrow shot by ... well, you can guess. Instantly a swarm of incensed bees were upon us, ready to exact stinging retribution. We ran. The bees followed me to my house and went inside as I ran through the door. My mother, sensing disaster, began shouting. I was petrified... but the bees, somehow sensing they had met their match when my mom opened her mouth, exited promptly. Nothing supernatural about it; those bees knew better than to anger my mother. In my childhood mind-set, I thought wow, my mother can rule the bees.

It wasn't wild and crazy all the time, but even the productive activities I got involved in became controversial. For example, one of my first jobs was as a morning newspaper delivery boy. That was not unusual; many kids my age delivered newspapers. My route was sizable. But in my case, I also wound up in an activity known then and today as "running numbers". One of my newspaper customers was a bookie. Rapidly I got acquainted with plain little brown envelopes, which I passed out to customers along with their newspapers. My periodic reward was $50 cash, sometimes more; depending on how many of my customers hit on a number. It was a veritable king's ransom for a tyke like me. It all came to an end when the state began a lottery of its own. Moral questions not withstanding, I was disappointed and irked, especially since they were doing the same thing I was doing, just on TV.

The $50 or so made me a "rich kid" who could do what he wanted. Step dad came into the picture too. When I came home from collecting on my paper route, he would confiscate most of my earnings and call it rent. Perhaps in his own awkward way he was trying to teach me responsibility, but it came across to this little guy as "taxation without representation." Eventually I wised up and began 'losing' customers... at least for step dad's information. Fortunately he never attempted to investigate, so my ploy worked.

Several dangerously winding streets adjoining Chartiers Avenue proved an irresistible lure for us kids both in summer and winter. In summer, we would ride our wagons at high speeds. The fact that our 'run' was also heavily traveled by both car and pedestrian traffic only added to the excitement. One day as usual, my half-brother and I kissed caution goodbye and sailed down the hill. Next to the sidewalk were tall, well manicured hedges. A wheel fell off my wagon, sending us off the sidewalk. For a brief euphoric moment, my stepbrother, myself and the groceries went sailing high over the hedges. With us we had two full bags of groceries. Unannounced and unwelcome, we "visited" a garden party. On the other side, a prim and proper garden party was in full swing. We were unwelcome for at least two reasons — improper dress for polite society and the fact that we disrupted the heck out of the party. We picked up our groceries and went home.

In winter, the routine was pretty much the same only with sleds. Forming sled trains, we raced on separate streets to a suicidal connecting point. We always managed to lose several sleds along the way, mostly at a nasty ninety-degree curve. At one time or another everyone got hurt — everybody except me — a real irony compared to my adult life. The adults that lived on the street where we held our sled races became our unexpected allies. For them it was great fun watching our death defying antics. When they knew we were going to do sled races, they would hose down the streets to provide... well... speed. Soon we were racing madly on pure ice.

This went on until one fateful day when an accident near the bottom of our suicide track ended our fun forever. That day, instead of connecting at the bottom with laughing friends eager to try it again, police awaited us. One friend had nearly sheared his arm off after hitting a guardrail. The authorities were less than amused. Knowing that forbidding us to sled ride on those streets would be useless, they took preventative measures and salted our track every single day it got below freezing. Each day the sun would set and I would have to go back to that house on Chartiers Avenue. I had to cope with the fact that a war zone awaited me, one that was unknown to the rest of the City of Pittsburgh and the world. It was all too real for me.

While we were generally regarded as mischievous and not harmless, our idea of fun included tying oppositely parked cars tail pipes together! It was not fun for either car owner.

I came to realize that, under my stepfather, an actual infraction of house rules was not necessary. All of us were subject to punishment for not only actual misbehavior but also perceived upcoming violations. No one escaped his wrath. Carol felt that he was a little more "compassionate" with his stepdaughters. With them the physical violence was more back of the hand stuff than closed fist. He was more apt to use verbal assaults on the girls.

I had an unenviable spot on my stepfather's hit list. As it was, my stepfather's imagination was an active place, operating round the clock and always vigilant to something to be angry about. It didn't help matters that I was determined to test limits. Intense physical beatings were simply a part of the picture. He was an equal opportunity idiot. He beat his own kids too.

An ironic twist was added to our already bent out of shape relationship. For a long time I was not aware that Andy was not my biological father. A friend of mine pointed out in his very best young kid's genealogical expertise that my last name was different from the last name of my step dad. So much for critical information in my life. Next time I'll pay closer attention.

Some families have appliances that malfunction with regularity. I came from a family that malfunctioned with regularity, because the captain of the ship had an irreparable, broken moral compass. We could all count on being punished… if not on a daily basis, at least every other day. It was a true conversation piece when the abuse was limited to verbal. In our home the most forbidden of "crimes" was crying, no matter how valid the reason. "I catch you crying and I'll give you a real reason to cry" was dear stepfather's verdict.

When I discovered my first real girl friend (I'll call her Laura), it was a slice of heaven. I valued my friends, but Laura was a treasure. I realized that neither Laura nor my friends could ever spend any significant amount of time in my home. Any visits that did occur were counted in nervous seconds or minutes.

Sarcasm and humor were employed extensively to help overcome the madness that surrounded us. My logic in dealing with it all became very simple if not crude; if we were going to be punished regardless, why not make the crime fit the punishment?

This led to an episode I'll call the "Venetian Blinds Affair." I had plans for that day—a date as I recall—with the childhood love of my life, Laura. At the last minute my stepfather, without apology, pulled the plug on my date. He may have had the power, but not the control. I had a job to do and it couldn't wait. The Venetian blinds in my parents' bedroom needed cleaning. With my stepfather, priorities were mostly based on how much of a sadistic thrill he could get from them.

This chore was no exception. Step dad expected the blinds to be taken down and cleaned. This thirteen year old was neither amused nor forgiving. But, I decided, the show must go on—and go on it did. I realized that I was "due" for a beating anyway. All beatings took place in the attic, a cramped area that myself and my brothers used as a bedroom. Calendars don't lie. It was punishment day. (Many families set aside days and times for specific chores and obligations;

we had "regular" punishment days). Knowing this, I decided to create a memorable infraction.

That evening, as ordered, the Venetian Blinds did get cleaned. They were hosed down--from inside the house !!! I dragged the hose upstairs to the second floor bedroom where my parents slept; then I let the water gush. Rugs, curtains, my parents' bed — this was an equal opportunity dousing. Everything in squirting distance got a bath—but the Venetian blinds did get cleaned. My half-brother was just returning home. He saw the sopping aftermath, which was sure to generate fireworks. Suddenly he remembered an important appointment elsewhere —anywhere.

In truth my mother was not above throwing a few blows of her own. She had small fists and long fingernails. She would hit you more if she broke one hitting you. I had an almost mysterious knack for saying things that got me into trouble. My mother had a saying she used when she was at the end of her rope and about to lose her considerable temper. She always began: "I am SICK and TIRED . . ."

One day, I brought on myself some deserved punishment for an act that escapes me now. Mom came roaring in with her verbal "judge's gavel" — "I am SICK . . .," she began angrily and she paused. The imp in me could not be suppressed. I turned to her like a game show host teasing a losing contestant and added with flair, "And tired . . . ". Instantly it was the Fourth of July. And she didn't slap, she punched. Those small fists were like acupuncture needles.

Once when I had a bad tooth, my stepfather tried his hand at dentistry. Out came a pair of pliers and moments later a tooth involuntarily left my mouth. Step dad proved to be largely a failure at homespun dentistry.

First, he was only marginally successful at stopping the bleeding in my mouth. Second, he may have pulled the wrong tooth. My pain- sensing system worked fine, based on the pain that erupted in my mouth. I never looked at a pair of pliers in the same way again.

Like most of my friends, I was a rambunctious, tree climbing kid. My tree climbing talents gave birth to an episode I called "The Horribly Swollen Foot" or "The Good Year Limp." I jumped out of a tree near my backyard and landed on a rusty nail sticking out of a board. I don't know how I missed seeing it. My mistake cost me dearly. It hurt and I bled. My stepfather, proving that there was no end to the perverse depths of his resourcefulness, launched his own version of podiatry. My foot was plunked into Epsom salts and left to soak. No other medical attention was forthcoming. The foot swelled quickly to grotesque proportions the size of a pineapple. As expected, my movement was severely limited. I adapted by learning to walk on my hands and knees for a year. I missed enough school to fail the fourth grade. I also wore the knees out of my pants.

I heard the word gangrene used to describe my foot condition. My stepfather's medical ingenuity continued. Displeased by the now gargantuan size of my foot, this aspiring Dr. Frankenstein administered a razor blade to the swollen area. Step dad's technique predated concerns of sterilization. (One took one's pain "like a man".) Once the razor broke skin, the pus shot out of my foot and hit the wall. The sight was unappetizing enough — then there was the matter of the smell. I am surprised I didn't lose my foot altogether.

My stepfather had a theory that beating you made you smarter. This occurred during "study periods" at home when I was trying to learn spelling. With each misspelling my stepfather barked "WRONG" in my ear, followed by a punch to the head. My head would ricochet off the wall. It became hazardous to misspell a word. Worse, poor step dad's efforts produced the opposite of the desired effect. To this day I cannot spell, even ignoring the limitations of my paralysis and other injuries.

To be fair, my stepfather did initiate and actively participate in a "family" style game involving belts and buckles. I have seen this snapping game being played in shower rooms with towels as weaponry. It was less fun when the brass end of the buckle connected with either bare or protected skin, as was the object of this game. I had the black and blue marks to prove it.

Other family fun included a bizarre mealtime ritual wherein we sat bolt upright at attention for the entire meal. No elbows on the table. When we went visiting, if we stayed for meals, it was bolt upright at the table — not just at first, but throughout the meal. This mandatory ritual prompted more than one strange stare from our hosts. My stepfather was unfazed. Discipline had to be maintained, even when it served no useful purpose.

Osteopathy was another field attempted by my stepfather. I remember at least one situation well. Step dad, Andy Jr. and I were playing ball in the lot near our house. Andy got hit in the nose with the ball, a direct result of my foul tip. The game took a time out due to player injury. It appeared that Andy Jr. had broken his nose and would require medical treatment. Step dad had a much more efficient approach. He strode up to Andy Jr., grabbed his nose between thumb and forefinger and yanked abruptly, theoretically straightening Andy Jr.'s nose. The nose did return to a semblance of normal but now it was twisted to the right. For a long time I kidded Andy Jr. that he looked liked he was signaling for a right turn.

I was secretly terrified of this short, stocky man who was so morally bankrupt. Later I would realize how much I missed having a constructive father figure. Conversations I have had with people from "healthy" families merely served to reinforce this point. Much of what went on under our roof at Chartiers Avenue during those grueling years would have earned my stepfather a jail term today. My sister Carol agrees quickly and forcefully. My collaborator for this project and I have chosen to be discreet about which horrors that occurred should be included in this retelling.

It's not that the abuses went unchallenged. On several occasions both Carol and I saw my mother attempt to intervene on our behalf. Her valor was rewarded by Andy forcefully punching her in the face, leaving her crumpled on the floor. I fear that the savage kicks to her ribs that followed may have caused her to rethink intervention. During one confrontation, he gave me a piece of "friendly family advice" that made my blood run cold. I threatened subtly to blow the whistle on his antics. Step dad told me calmly and pointedly that if anyone ever found out what went on inside our house, I would be the first to die. Given his savage and unpredictable track record, I was not inclined to take that advice lightly.

Age thirteen was to be a major milestone in my life because of an occurrence in the dreaded attic. I was enduring one of many in an eternal series of beatings. My stepfather administered them with enthusiasm and a perverse dedication. As the blows rained down, I had finally had ENOUGH! The fear, rage and hate that had boiled in me for so long finally exploded. I fought back and won.

It was a spontaneous, vicious scene that made me feel great at the time as well as today. It was inevitable. Though only a kid, my natural height and physique weighed in my favor. The oppressor vanquished; I left the attic. Considering the sight that greeted me immediately after, my victory was hollow indeed. I still have visions of that moment, of my mother, reduced to a trance like state, sucking her thumb as she huddled with the children in the stairway. This once strong, respectable woman had been reduced to a shell, courtesy of a rabid wolf in sheep's clothing; a sinister servant of which Satan surely was proud.

I have had more than one opportunity to reflect back on that horrific turning point. Here was the "father" of the family, a dangerously obsessive disciplinarian who brought my mom, my brothers and sisters, and others, literally to their knees. Now he had been bested by a thirteen year old in a desperate situation. Whatever credibility for manhood or integrity I might have grudgingly given him was blown away in that victory.

Years later, to those whom I related the incident, the verdict was unanimous. I should have killed the SOB. The fact is that my stepfather died years later of natural causes (assuming anything about my stepfather could be considered natural). Since becoming a Christian I have forgiven him, but I reserve the right not to mourn or miss him! If I'm wrong to hold negative memories of my step dad, I'll take it up with the Almighty. If He insists on me saying something nice about my stepfather, I can say he was a great cook and prepared a number of truly delicious meals. That makes his resume as a human being a trifle less lopsided.

The situation was now clearly intolerable; I left home. I lived briefly with Carol and her new husband, Ed Wolf. Ed and Carol lived only a mile from my home. That was just far enough to be out of the line of fire. My new surroundings were far more hospitable and infinitely safer. Improved though my new situation was, it could not be a permanent solution. But, thank God, it was a start.

Carol had intervened on my behalf numerous times, reducing my punishments from unbearable and possibly life threatening to mere torture. Now, Carol, along with Ed, would have a long-term influence on my life that was as valuable and needed as it was wonderful. I guess they and the Lord forgave the teenager in me for taking their early hospitality a bit for granted.

Ed Wolf
"Truly One of the Great Ones"

In the Wolf household there was more generosity in their hearts than food on their table. A nasty detail kept cropping up; not enough food to go around, especially with children added to the picture. Limited though their resources were, the question of sharing was rarely an issue. One time 'the Wolf' padlocked the refrigerator and wrapped a chain around it. It was a fact that an active teenager consumes food and drink like a vacuum cleaner.

My musical talents surfaced when I would invite myself to join impromptu street corner quartets who were harmonizing. The majority of these singers were black and damned good at keeping that tune. My newfound musical colleagues made an amazing discovery —I was good.

Another aspect of my character that reared its ugly head was my temper. It took no more than a few poorly chosen words on the part of the other person and Jim Crosson's fists were flying. My physique was taking on manly dimensions, which improved my chances of winning these impulsive street fights. Along with the physique, a nickname, J. C., short for James Crosson, was taking root and would follow me throughout my life. (Take note of the extreme irony here.)

At times during my stay with "The Wolf", I shook things up unintentionally. For example, I had painted the gas tank from my motorcycle a sweet candy apple red. To dry the paint, I washed out the tank with water (mistake #1) and then placed it in the oven (mistake #2) to give it a baked finish. The door blew open, my sister almost had a heart attack, and Ed just stood there.

Not because of this incident, but I sometimes slept outside the Wolf home in a '55 Ford station wagon. I realized that the Wolf household was too crowded to comfortably accommodate another active person. Carol and Ed needed time to themselves. They were, after all, still pretty much newlyweds.

Arguments would sometimes break out between The Wolf and myself. None of these arguments were hostile because we loved and respected each other. In fact it was Ed Wolf who bought me my first car, a '53 Chevy Convertible. Our disagreements did have the potential to become nasty, given enough time and pressure. And for some peculiar but not at all unwelcome reason, attractive young ladies found my motel-on-wheels intriguing and irresistible. Who was I to argue?

I would like to talk about Ed for a moment. He was an entrepreneur. We formed a partnership in the aluminum siding business among other ventures. When I was home on leave from the Marine Corps, we made a brief foray into the furnace repair business. We took one lady's furnace apart and couldn't get it back together. The original reason for our "service call" had been laughably simple. I think we were just supposed to clean the furnace. We had parts strewn everywhere. The lady became both concerned and suspicious. Wolf had to call a close friend, who was an actual furnace man, to bail us out.

This tall, balding (thanks to me, I'm told) guy with the angular face and quiet disposition was a bit of a contradiction. To some he was a schemer and a flim-flam man, but yet unfailingly popular. Even when you were mad at The Wolf, you liked him. His funeral years later was enormous, roughly what might be expected from a celebrity. He was a childlike, innocent man who was addicted to homemade chocolate chip cookies and Walt Disney characters. A Mickey Mouse likeness adorns his tombstone.

Together we worked on cars and chatted for hours. Ed Wolf was not only one of my greatest friends but he served as a father figure. My time spent with the Wolf household was a fantastic time. It was a critical bridge between escaping from the hell that was my home and searching for a more peaceful existence.

Eventually it became painfully obvious that the Wolf household could not support five people. It was time to make an important decision – it was best that I moved on.

Now the streets of New York City became home. My stepfather's mother lived there. Central Park became my living room. The Missions kept me from starving. Readers today, and especially those familiar with New York City and environs circa 2000, may correctly tend to assume that I was either a bit suicidal or at least a little crazy to live like that. But New York City was a different place in the early '60s.

The Big Apple had its share of danger, but it was never a lethal jungle. I was tall, muscular, and rugged and this may have discouraged those of evil intent. Some of the derelicts were friendly and entertaining, even charming, not unlike what one might see in a Broadway musical. I learned how to turn dumpster diving for throwaway food from classy restaurants into a decent meal. (What will it be tonight? Italian or Chinese?) I learned to keep my friends close and my enemies closer.

I could see no evidence that God was working in my life. Then again, I found no need for God so I wasn't on the lookout for His works. In Jim Crosson's mind, God was wisely keeping his distance. I always thought of God as an old guy in the sky that said 'happy birthday' once a year. I had no idea how much I was depending on him. I never thought He did anything for me; I thought I did it on my own.

While my mind was miles from spiritual concerns, that did not keep a dogged spiritual purpose from being weaved into my life. This Higher Power, who had been keeping a careful eye on me, had realized that a hardened street kid who was convinced that he could count on no one but himself could not be approached directly. So He slipped in inconspicuously. I should be thankful for my "security apses". However, daily survival was my primary concern. Lyrics from a Sinatra song played in my consciousness. Something like 'if you could make it in New York City, you could make it anywhere.' In hindsight, I tend to agree with Ol' Blue Eyes.

Blessings appeared quietly in the form of a part time job in a print shop. My stepfather's mother assisted where she could. She let me live with her. I came to realize that because one person in a family was a psycho, everyone else was not a suspect. My stepfather's mother understood the situation. She had harsh words for her son but could do nothing to change him. Thus, she was eager to help me.

Yes, He does work in strange and mysterious ways. For example, it was my stepfather's mother who helped get me a print shop job in Mineola, Long Island. The print shop had certifiably ancient equipment. The money didn't hurt either.

This street kid was still a confirmed rebel (a rebel without a clue) but he was under 'spiritual construction'. But, the progress could only be seen under a magnifying glass!

Time passed. My life took on a routine. The war zone on Chartiers Avenue was history, at least for me. Carol had left first when she married. I was second. Candy followed shortly afterward. My two stepbrothers stayed much longer for reasons best known to them. For me, it was a question of what next.

I lived and worked in New York City for about a year before coming back to Pittsburgh. A waiting job and a worth waiting- for-young lass brought me back home. The job was in a grocery store. The more important attraction was named Shirley. I was never at a loss for female companionship, either as just friends or intimate companions. Today, I look back and regret not handling the relationships with more respect.

I once again moved in with Ed and Carol Wolf. This time a newly discovered nuisance called a 'conscience' was on my mind. As a Higher Power looked on, I paid Ed and Carol all I could afford; it was not nearly enough to cover their hospitality, but part of my spiritual construction was bearing fruit.

Spiritual construction can take a while, especially when bad attitudes are firmly entrenched. I put my hosts through tests of fire, but with better intentions and better results. I was making progress. On this visit Ed Wolf helped me secure a motorcycle, my pride and joy. I guess I had been forgiven for the episode when I borrowed his car, accidentally broke off the driver's door and returned the vehicle "intact".

I stalled the Wolf's car on a hill. Letting it drift backward to catch it into gear seemed a practical solution. The car got away from me. A telephone pole, which had been lurking nearby, sheared off the driver's door. Using the always reliable Crosson street genius, I carefully put the door back on without actually repairing it and returned the car. It looked fine but it just wasn't connected to the hinges! It was the following morning when a blissfully unaware Ed Wolf yanked on his car door to go to work only to have the entire door fall on his foot!!!

My name, adorned with an epithet or two, echoed for several minutes throughout the neighborhood. Such was the price of friendship with me.

Another close friend who warrants mention is one Louie Nickerson. Actually the late Louie Nickerson. Louie and I had been the closest of friends throughout school. He was a lovable oddball who helped keep my spirits up during some tough times. It may have been Louie, of all people, who helped me to realize that there were those people I could relax with and trust. We took trips together, worked legitimate jobs together and got into trouble together. We did everything, moral and immoral, legal and illegal, ethical and unethical. The fact that we were gutsy helped save our backsides on numerous occasions, particularly on a hair-raising trip to Florida.

Curiously reminiscent of the famous classic John Belushi movie "The Blues Brothers", we left for Florida with a full tank of gas and $30 between us. A plan—what plan— who needed a plan? In Florida we picked oranges, stayed with migrant workers and pumped gas. Those migrant workers could out pick us. So we looked for the biggest oranges. It happened to be on one of the trees was his prize-growing tree, which had won first prize in the county fair for three years straight. We turned in our pick of the day, got paid, and left immediately.

Our adventures were akin to something out of a Steinbeck novel except that the conditions were not nearly as harsh. But, we saw the military draft coming our way, so Louie and I joined the military on the same day. He couldn't qualify for the Marines because of his height but he did get into the Army. Both of us went to Vietnam. I came back alive.

Parts of my life that mattered now appeared to be maintaining an even keel. Soon, however, the lyrics to that old song, "been down so long it looks like up to me," would take on an eerie significance.

Chapter Two
J.C. vs. the U.S.M.C.

Some people leave home to go to the service. I left the back of a '55 Ford Wagon to join the Marines. There was no patriotism in my choice. Enlisting in the Marines was a matter of necessity. My goal was three square meals a day, nothing nobler than that. There was another complication. I joined when the Vietnam 'conflict' was heating up and the armed services, especially the Marines, needed warm bodies to send to Vietnam. As I left home so young, I had to quit school to join the Marines, but I got a G.E.D. in the Marine Corps, which means "Good Enough Diploma". I always viewed the Marine Corps as my first baptism; a baptism by fire.

Train them fast and send them over faster was the unwritten but necessary code of operations. The fact that I was unaware of this didn't keep me out of this high-powered meat grinder. My arrival at Boot Camp on Parris Island, South Carolina was less than auspicious. True to form, I was drunk and strutted off the bus with my most practiced "go to hell and tell them I sent you" attitude. Authority was something to be ignored. I had chips on both shoulders.

The Drill Instructor yelled, "You guys have four seconds to get off this bus, and three are gone already". He told me "Move you long-haired slob" and I took a swing at him because I didn't know any better. He beat the daylights out of me. My action was not brave, it was dumb.

Soon, I was confident; the Marine Corps would be at its knees in front of me. The powers of the drill instructors to read my thoughts were more than willing to prove me wrong. Basic training is tough enough without an attitude. I never imagined the Great Sculptor using bellowing drill sergeants and a dizzying number of pushups to help with my molding process. Yes, I was slowly, almost at glacial speed, being remolded into a Marine. For significant others in my life, the finished product could not come too soon.

One hears glorious stories of wayward lads donning the colors of the Marine Corps and being transformed forthwith into responsible, respectable young men. None of those stories had me in mind. My rocky past and perfected antagonistic attitude were to be my downfall for some time to come. I tell people that I went into the Marines with nothing and came out with nothing. I guess I wasn't looking for "nothing."

Only moments off the bus, my relationship with the Marine Corps was defined. The drill sergeant "welcomed" us at a volume level generally reserved for the severely hearing impaired. He was fresh out of compliments but had an endless supply of insults that he was aching to use.

The Marine Corps is a good institution. I am NOT criticizing the Corps. Their job was to break you down and rebuild you. The commercial says we want a few good men, and I was currently not one of them.

Back to the ill-conceived punch I threw at the D.I. I went down hard but I was determined to get the number of that truck. Normal caution and logic dictated that any sane person would stay still and shut up. I never had any use for normal caution and logic. To settle the score, I jumped the drill sergeant from behind. Once again, I discovered how hard, fast and how often he could hit. At the time I looked at my actions as an unprecedented act of bravery. It didn't take long for me to see my actions for what they were—foolhardy. Could our irritable "host" have been suffering from PMS?—possibly wrong gender PMS? Whatever the case, I was officially a member of Platoon #284.

Standing at attention for lengthy periods of time was a matter of fond priority with the Marines. It doesn't much matter whether one was standing at attention in the barracks or any other damn place. This and other "torture" exercises actually served a purpose, we were told. As I noted before, new recruits had to be forcefully and quickly torn down both in emotions and attitudes so we could be rebuilt, both body and soul, in the image of the Marine Corps. The purpose was to instill the discipline to follow orders instantly and without question; (e. g., to stay perfectly stiff should we need to do so in order not to reveal our position to the enemy.) So both the Lord and the Marine Corps were attempting to remold me from what was admittedly a difficult street kid. I wonder who had the harder job?

The Marines are great for helping one learn trivial information. I learned, for example, why the Mess Hall was so named. The reason was simple: the food is dumped out in a mess.

In fine restaurants, diners are encouraged to take their time and savor the cuisine. Since there is no cuisine to be "savored" in the Mess Hall, recruits are required to eat against the stopwatch. Five minutes was maximum eating time and everyone had to start eating in unison. Dessert was conspicuously absent from the menu. There was an ad campaign that insisted: "There's always room for Jell-O". It never took the Mess Hall into account.

I am a naturally slow eater—always have been—so I was destined for trouble. During my first three days of Boot Camp, I went on an unplanned "diet." My long-standing eating habit was to sort the food served to me. In Boot Camp, this cost me eating time. At the same moment I was taking my first bite of food, it was time for us to leave—as a group. Hence I got little food for the first three days.

I quickly adjusted to eating in several large gulps. From a practical standpoint, this lends itself to puddings or liquid meals. I had to teach my eyes to lie to my stomach ... and just swallow. It was also customary to protect your silverware. (This caused a minor stir later when I was home on leave and ate with my girlfriend's parents. A plaintive question arose: "Where's all the silverware?" No problem. J. C. (my nickname) had it carefully hidden by his plate. Mystery solved.)

Once we had to stand at rigid attention against the end of our bunks in our barracks. This lasted three hours. Some of the biggest bruisers collapsed early. I held out to the end only because I cheated a little. Marine Corps issue pants always have belts that are too long. It is up to the recruit to cut their belts to fit. I hadn't cut mine yet, so I looped the belt around my chest and my bunk. It gave me welcome support. Watching other recruits' reactions to the merciless grilling that was basic training, I came to a conclusion — "Well adjusted" guys that came from "good homes" fared the worst! I was almost grateful for my twisted upbringing.

Regarding basic training, I have told various people that: "If you went in crazy, you were one step ahead." This is not nearly the exaggeration the reader might assume. The Marines have a fetish for pushups. Once, when I was being punished with pushups, the drill sergeant had an interesting statement: "You do pushups until I get tired."

Other Marine pastimes were marching and running. Seven days a week, as often as possible, run and march. To their credit, the Drill Instructors ran alongside us, rain or shine, "urging" us on, making us sing explicit adult lyrics that guys our age could identify with easily. The Marines wanted us to (actually we needed to for our safety) react on instinct. There is no time for intellectual discourse or contemplation on the field of battle when the hot lead is flying.

Forced marches in any conditions were standard. One day we did our run through a drenching downpour; five miles had never been this long. At the end of this glorious communion with nature was an obstacle course beginning with a tall vertical device. This "ladder" or "obstacle" was part of a large and complex course. It earned itself a nickname among us recruits: We called it "Big Bertha." Nature, yes, I thought…, but this was getting out of hand. It was still pouring and mud was accumulating on the rungs when I started up the adder. I slipped and fell to the ground flat on my back. I didn't even have a chance to call time out when Mr. Megaphone was in my face screaming "YOU AINT DEAD, YOU'RE STILL SUCKING AIR, BOY, GET UP!" It was not in the cards for us to become best friends, I guess.

It didn't even seem to matter that we lost a man on one of the midnight swamp marches. His next of kin got a form letter. The casualty was referred to in later lectures as "alligator bait". Today the incident would not be dispatched as easily.

Some people are overweight when they go into the Marines. Nobody leaves the Marines overweight; insane perhaps, but never overweight. Recruits who were overweight faced a tougher road than others. They were called "Fatbodies", a derisive label that stayed with them regardless of how well they shaped up. They were permitted no desserts and generally were the butt of extensive humiliation.

At the completion of basic, the recruit's body is well honed and totally fit. Whether or not said recruit liked the training is another matter. It would be grossly unfair of me to take jabs at Marine Corps training without giving the other side of the story. For those of us who made it through, basic training made us tough and disciplined. We agreed that the toughness and discipline instilled in us definitely saved lives in Vietnam. On every field of battle, but especially in the madness that was Vietnam, toughness and discipline provided stability in situations that would normally lend themselves to panic and confusion.

No recounting of basic training would be complete without a glimpse of the rifle range. All recruits were required to train on the rifle range. The rifle range was the make-you-or- break-you test of the Marine Corps. A recruit who scored poorly on the rifle range would wish he were never born. One thing was for certain — the Marines would not hold him in high regard. Doing poorly on the rifle range even had an official slang name. It was called "going unk." If the recruit missed the target, he not only lost points, his error was registered by a red flag, known to recruits as "Maggie's Drawers."

It was necessary to use proper terminology. For example, recruits did not refer to the long fighting instrument that spews bullets as a "gun"; the proper term is "rifle." Allow me a moment to brag. I did very well on the rifle range. In fact, I have a medal that reads "Rifle Expert". I could hit a beer can at 100 yards with open sites. There were no shortcuts in this one. I earned that award and still hold it in high regard today.

Amateur boxing briefly caught my eye while in basic training. I used my height and strength to considerable and frequent advantage, towering over most of my opponents and pummeling them. I was a power puncher. For a short time, I was 'The Champ'. I won a fair number of contests. 'All fair in love and war' was my attitude. This boxing career was never to see the lights of Madison Square Garden, due in large part to a match I had with a little Filipino sergeant. I figured this 'runt' would be just another notch in my already impressive belt. We were in our respective corners, waiting for the bell to ring. I heard the bell, and then the next thing I remember was someone helping me off the mat. Apparently the 'runt' had leapt across the ring with lightning speed and rained down a series of blows; I was never beaten up so bad and so fast. It was after this match that my boxing career ended. Power punching means nothing when faced with such speed.

Teenagers are often reprimanded about slamming doors. One morning I walked into the Mess Hall and, without thinking, let the screen door slam. The sound echoed throughout the hall. I thought nothing of it until my favorite drill sergeant appeared in my face. My punishment would have made environmentalists happy. I had to go outside to the nearest tree and apologize verbally and at length for waking it out of its slumber. Should my apology be rejected, all would not be lost; this lumbering giant could get a whole new life as paper products.

There were the lighter moments too. I received a tin of cookies from my sister at home. The Drill Sergeant "asked" (told) me if I intended to share my gift with him. My response was in the negative; points lost. He asked me why I did not intend to share my gift with him. I told him truthfully but bluntly. I even added "sir." Sarge made me eat the entire tin of cookies, immediately, without water. My lips and mouth were bleeding when the final cookie went down.

While in the Basic Training, attitude not withstanding, my street savvy worked in my favor. An aptitude test told the Marines I would do well in demolition, although demolition was not nearly the precise science it has become today. It was more like a farmer blowing up a tree stump. There were no controlled implosions... nothing technical. We identified it, we blew it up. I was sentimental too. I would always take a picture of a bridge before we turned it into debris.

The Marine Corps and I were often at cross-purposes. But I want to give credit where credit is due. The Marines are a fine outfit. For all the friction I lived through/created, I have nothing negative to say about the Marine Corps. But, like mismatched lovers, we were simply not meant for each other. I tell people that the Marines were looking for a few good men. I simply was not one of them!

The Marines do what they have to do. Often their methods save lives in the unpredictable hell of battle. I saw some truly tough guys wash out of basic. It is curious to me that I did not. But for me, even at its worst, Basic Training was like a day at home with my stepfather... except that these people had uniforms and I couldn't just leave if I wanted to.

The experiences I have described are from the old Marine Corps, which was, I'm told, much tougher than current day Marine training. People who should know have told me that training is much more "sensitive" these days.

I had no way of knowing that a much tougher test for me was just around the corner. Like most of what happened to me in the military, this test was not a matter of choice. I was headed into a state of disruption. A much Higher Power was fortunately preparing to help me through it.

Chapter Three
Good Morning, Viet Nam

I read the Marines have a high mortality rate. I did not expect to make it back, so I took a bus ride to California to see as much of America as I could before the end.

I was a shutterbug, but that turned out to be a dangerous hobby. I would point my camera at beautiful hills or even a sensitive military target, and — ping, ping, ping — came the whiz of bullets around my head. I tried to take it all in stride by developing a safe routine. I would aim my camera, snap quickly, hear — ping, ping, ping — , roll for cover, stay low for a while and repeat the operation. One does what one has to do in a war zone.

I've discovered firsthand that war does strange things to people. Some guys came in with timid attitudes; at best they blended into the woodwork. I'm sure none of them suspected it but they would all change. "Yellow streaks became mean streaks" to quote myself. Guys who had been in 'the bush' too long (as most of Vietnam was called) developed a certain look. The look was difficult to describe but was unmistakable to Marines. It was called "looking beyond" or "the glare". This stare was not to be taken lightly. It was as if my fellow Marines were looking well beyond their surroundings to a place the rest of us could not see. They were looking death, destruction and suffering in the eye. When you had the "looking beyond" stare, death meant nothing. You were numb to pain. Death or insanity were the only other options.

After two tours of duty, I told the guys in my platoon I was so short that I can't have a long conversation. Before I went to Vietnam, I hadn't killed anything. I didn't hate the Viet Cong for ethnic or even philosophical reasons; I hated them for what they made me become.

Vietnam was not a prime location for the sensitive artist. Drug usage was commonplace. I smoked my share of marijuana, as we all did. Readers, and specifically the Christian readership for which this is intended, will have to be open-minded. Survival demands exercising options that at other times would never be considered.

Lighter moments did occur — packages from home for instance. In history we read about the 'shot heard round the world'. I was a party to the 'gift heard round the base' at east. Carol sent an innocent package. It was white and square. She had placed a gutter spike in the middle of it to prevent it being crushed in transit. A gutter spike is basically a large glorified nail with a protective covering. That alone would not have created a problem except that one side of the box had been smashed, exposing the spike. Now the package was suspect. I recognized Carol's handwriting, but rules were rules. The cry went out: BOOBY TRAP! Demolition man Crosson and his trusty band of bang-up associates took the white box out to an empty field to examine it further, but most likely to detonate it. Carefully, ever so carefully, we opened it. Then the cry went up with equal fervor: CAKE! Yes, Cake. As in… birthday... cake.

The rest of my company swarmed the cake. A moment later it was gone—devoured. Silverware was not required, especially when fingers were available. I'm sure Carol expected me to share my cake but not to the point of self sacrifice.

Shortly before my tour of duty was to end, my life changed dramatically.

After two tours, I had exactly thirty-eight days to go before I exited the hell hole on earth. The number thirty-eight would come to have special meaning for me. It was the day when the bottom fell out of my life. Like we said in Nam, 38 days and a wake-up!

The incident began with what should have been a simple trip to the field with Marine engineers. It was September 23, 1968. The purpose of our mission was to clear and mines. It would be pure irony. Two vehicles went out that day, a jeep and a six-ton dump truck. I brought up the rear driving the truck. My truck was the heaviest truck used by the Corps. Six men on foot walked alongside my truck. Earlier in the day, I had sandbagged the truck. (Sandbagging refers to a protective reinforcement of a vehicle in which sandbags are packed closely together beneath the floorboards to blunt the impact of an explosion.) It was a lot of work and, at the time, I did not know that God had a hand in having me go through such an ordeal. It would prove to save my life.

Ahead of me, the jeep carried portable mine detectors which would signal the discovery of any metal mine. Plastic mines, every bit as deadly as metal mines, also existed. The jeep passed over one without incident. My truck was heavier. Beneath my truck, a sixty-pound plastic antitank land mine detonated with a fury. The six men surrounding my truck died.

I was blown completely from the truck and onto the road next to a rice paddy. I must have suffered a concussion since part of my diagnosis was head trauma. Either minutes or an eternity later, I was crawling in a daze on my hands and knees on the road where the truck should have been.

Around me was the familiar ping, ping, ping of automatic weapons fire. I could see dirt kicked up. The Viet Cong were taking full advantage of the chaos. A nearby Corpsman ran through a hail of bullets, risking his own life, and threw me over the embankment. The Corpsman was the unsung medical hero for the marines in Vietnam. The Viet Cong retreated into their tunnels to avoid being spotted from the air. The Corpsman used what was left of my M-14 rifle to splint my eg. I was evacuated by helicopter to a medical facility called an 'evac hospital', which had half-moon shaped Quonset huts (instead of the MASH tents everyone remembers from TV). That corpsman is the unsung hero of a lot Marines.

In another act of divine intervention, a friend of mine had borrowed my camera to take some pictures for himself. He took pictures of the truck, the accident scene, and the debris. That is how the camera, which had been on my person, was not blown up with me. Those very pictures which are in this book, were taken with that very camera. My friend and comrade was given the inspiration to borrow the camera, take the pictures, preserve them in battle, and send them to me. You tell me that the hand of God was not on him and me.

Because of my head injury, I could not be given pain medication. So they sewed up my face 'au naturale'. The speedometer from my truck wound up in my mouth, literally. It did so forcibly, removing a number of my teeth in the process. It would leave a strange scar as its calling card. Another souvenir I brought home was a right forearm full of shrapnel. It resides there to this day.

My ribs were broken and my ankles were shattered. And I was the least injured of the crew. A doctor who was examining me noted that a round was still in the firing chamber of my rifle, which was still strapped to my leg. Casually, he ejected it as though it were part of everyday routine and snorted "them damn Marines."

Jimmy Crosson, shutterbug, had loaned his prize camera to a fellow Marine on that fateful trip. He snapped vivid pictures of my truck after the explosion — well, what was left of my truck... My prize vehicle was near unrecognizable. The explosion had, among other restructuring, sent the engine flying several hundred feet down the road.

The object in evac was to "get 'em fixed up fast and out of there." The medical patching process earned the name "meatball surgery," an affectionate term for dealing with a horrible situation the best way possible.

CROSSON'S TRUCK - VIET-NAM
After hitting 60 lb. Land Mine

In the hours that followed, medical reports with my name on them were not promising. A death certificate was prepared. Had I been looking at someone else's injury report, I would have come to the same hopeless conclusion.

But, a Higher Power had other plans for me and chose to intervene. This Guardian Angel that I only peripherally believed in insisted on being there during life's most horrific moments. Today I readily and thankfully acknowledge God's loving and protective touch that led me to sandbag the truck, lessening the chances of becoming a fatality. Never again will I take lightly the axiom, "It's in God's hands."

Military shorthand involving colored stickers was used to indicate recovery status. These stickers were attached to the beds of recuperating soldiers. White meant that the patient was to be patched up and sent back into the field. A pink sticker earned one a permanent trip home. Soon a pink sticker adorned my bed. As far as the medical people were concerned, this ended my less than enthusiastic career in that far off country.

I was due a purple heart, one of the most honored and celebrated of medals. The Purple Heart has a special place among uniformed men. It is never regarded trivially. An orderly, apparently in charge of distributing medals, swung casually past my bed and dumped the Purple Heart on my chest as if he were returning a pack of cheap cigarettes. Only the fact that I was in traction and completely immobile saved this orderly from significant bodily injury that would have been administered by me. That medal meant something valuable to me. It was not a cheap carnival prize.

Perhaps the Purple Heart meant so much to me because I was due another medal, a Bronze Star, prior to this incident. Purple hearts signify official recognition for injuries received in the line of duty. Bronze stars are for bravery, whether or not one is injured. I was due the bronze star because I saved a truckload of fellow Marines when I realized that we were riding in a vehicle that was being hit by armor piercing bullets. When I saw the first of my comrades get shot, I leaped into action, emptying out the truck as fast as I could, thus saving lives. The Bronze Star I was rightfully promised for that action is still floating in military limbo, an area that too often gives a new meaning to the word slow.

In my life, freakish twists were commonplace. A classic example of this came while I lay in the EVAC hospital. Someone casually asked me what I thought of being in the Marines. Blithely I quipped "the Marines were the unwilling, led by the unqualified, to do the unnecessary," and dismissed the question. There were others who did not dismiss it as rapidly. Soon after, my quote wound up on the front page of "Stars and Stripes," the official military newspaper. My remarks had been noted and duly reported. I thought it was pretty fumy at the time until I got a visit from my superiors who insisted that my comments were ill considered and should not be repeated. And these people were in a position to insist.

From the EVAC field hospital I was taken to the nearby Da Nang Hospital which is closer to what we would call a regular medical facility; one with four walls. Da Nang hospital, I'm told, was a very competent facility but I have a sneaking suspicion that there were bright bulls-eyes painted on its roof. This bastion of mercy was shelled as often I got beaten at home.

It wasn't long before I was on a flight home, destined for 'recuperation'. I looked out the window and said " Goodbye Vietnam, you are nothing more than a bad memory…" It was the best thing I ever did… leave it behind.

The cargo plane had cots hanging from its walls, filled with the injured and maimed. An uncomfortable number of coffins were included also. When we landed in Bethesda, Maryland, there was no band... no flags... nobody.

Bethesda Naval Hospital would be where I would spend significant recuperation time. My stay was shorter than planned as the returning injured grew rapidly in number. The overflowing Bethesda Naval Hospital was glad to discharge those that were not in critical condition. I was one of those discharged for bed space.

It strikes me as odd now that I was discharged, since my injuries from the land mine were anything but minor. No matter. If one could breath, walk and get out of bed, one was expected to give up his bed for more life threatening cases. The government had an official term for sacrificing our beds. It was called convalescent leave, a polite way of saying, "go home and recover—we got no room for you here."

During 'recuperation', I was put to work in the basement of the Pentagon. In espionage fiction, the basement of the Pentagon often plays host to either of two extremes: super high tech clandestine operations or a dumping ground for embarrassing evidence. I helped mail form letters to the parents and next of kin of my fellow servicemen who would never again see the light of day.

This gruesome assignment took its toll on me emotionally. It was a dumb thing to make a Vietnam vet do. After only one day, I bailed out and joined my buddies on convalescent leave. Looking back over my short lived basement assignment, I realize this was one of few times that I did not choose to tough out a challenge. It was simply the wrong kind of challenge and at the worst possible time.

Stateside, public attitude toward the Vietnam War was at its height of unpopularity, creating a hostile climate, politically, socially and emotionally. I was unaware of this coming back. Officially, Vietnam was only a "conflict", since Congress had never declared it a war. For those who fought in this so-called "police action", we knew it was a war all too well.

I was to find out how intense this backlash was. I was sitting at a bar in Savannah, Georgia. My military uniform may have stood out more than was wise against the rest of the patrons' attire. I was on one of several "convalescent leaves" designed to help me put myself back together. My stay in this truly beautiful city in deep Dixie lasted scarcely a few days, but it left a permanent impression on me. Without warning, an unidentified man, crazy with hate against anyone wearing a uniform, stabbed me with a knife.

To antiwar protesters, the men in uniform were the epitome of evil; rapists, murderers, or, far worse, baby killers. We were unforgivable beasts who preyed upon the weakest of humanity overseas. The media had done us no favors, 'painting' vivid pictures from limited information.

Once again this headstrong kid, who still only knew God as a preface to the word 'damn,' was protected. My body cast stopped the knife's penetration, causing a small wound. Another miracle had occurred in my life.

My redneck assailant did not get off Scott-free. I grabbed him by the neck and for a brief moment, my boxing career returned. Angrily, I pummeled this big country boy, leaving him on a heap on the barroom floor. Then, dark humor would have its day. The knife he had stabbed me with was still sticking in me, bobbing back and forth. The bartender, as polite as can be, asked if we wouldn't mind leaving his establishment. My buddy and I left.

I went back to Bethesda Naval Hospital for a new cast, then they sent me home. After the period of recovery at home, I returned to the Marines. This time my home base was Camp Geiger, North Carolina. This is where you did time before a discharge.

After a dizzying series of promotions and demotions, I was now Sergeant of the Guard and had the privileges of that rank. I had been told more than once that, due to my innate intelligence, talent, and especially aggressiveness, I could have gone far in the Marines. My attitude guaranteed otherwise.

Being a Sergeant was very good to me. My rock band, Aladdin, was picking up serious steam. I was the only permanent member as other members came and went. We had an agent and got profitable bookings. We even played Las Vegas. (These adventures came under the classification of convalescent leave.) Booze, drugs and beautiful, compliant women were as available to me then as bad luck had been previously. The abundant supply of money was not unwelcome either. A majority of the Commandments were either broken or seriously dented. I thought I was invincible. But the lust of the flesh took marked priority over performing as agreed on stage. The band fell apart.

I also learned several permanent moral lessons as a direct result of my time with this band. The lust of the flesh and the lure of power and money can be all consuming and dangerously blinding. I went through seemingly inexhaustible amounts of money with horrifying speed. Then there were the drugs. Most if not all my illegal narcotics supply came directly from exceptionally reliable sources – the local police. I used to joke that I had low friends in high places.

As a Christian now, I am not proud of my exploits at that time, but they did occur, based on my moral values then. It serves now as a sharp and often uncomfortable reminder of how foolish a person can get. The how of this joyride is as darkly fascinating as the why.

Camp Geiger was also a stopping point for Marines who just finished boot camp. I bought some of the 'boots' beer so they would listen to my stories. The Officer of the Day (the OD) caught me in this forbidden activity and busted me to Lance Corporal on the spot.

My next adventure took me to Fort Stewart in Savannah, Georgia to demonstrate demolitions - how to use dynamite and C4. We had a few beers at the NCO club and went back to barracks to clean up for a jaunt into the nearby town. (it is important to note that on base, a Marine keeps his rifle with him at all times; if that were not possible, we would chain our rifles to any pole; note the chain) We went to the local American Legion and strolled through the front door. You were supposed to pay to enter. As our last guy went in, the doorman said, " Hey, you have to pay to come in here." Our last man turned and hit him in the face with the chain.

How stupid was that! I swear the music stopped dead. We were heavily outnumbered. The best choice was to exit. I ran for my life. Outside in the dark, I could see a light in the distance as I sprinted through a cornfield. The light was on a pole above a farmer's garage where he was working on his truck. I knocked on the door of the house not realizing it was 3 AM. The door inched open and a gun barrel poked out, just like in the cartoons. I ran back to the garage and begged for a ride back to town. A few dollars helped convince him. As we were driving back to base on a dirt road, we found one of my platoon members spread eagle in the road. I thought he was dead! As I knelt next to him and asked 'Are you ok? ', he quietly moaned, " I'm tired and I can't run no more…" We threw him in the back of the truck.

Next morning, the Army commanders ordered us to leave Fort Stewart. Returning in shame to Camp Geiger, we were restricted to base for two weeks. My discharge day was near. The day of my discharge, I received my papers, which curiously included a death certificate… processed the day I was injured by the landmine. I guess they didn't expect me to make it (few survive those explosions). I did.

The Far East

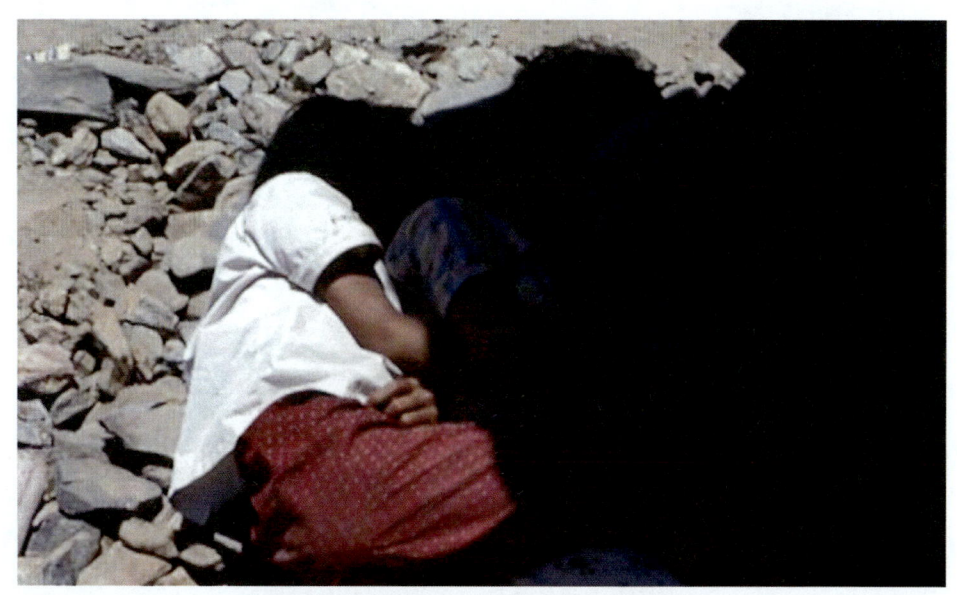

Little Children Sleeping on Rocks

Sunset at Gate One

Mine Sweeper Chi Mon Trail

Jim "Rambo" Crosson

My Platoon in 1967

Rice Paddy in Vietnam in 1967

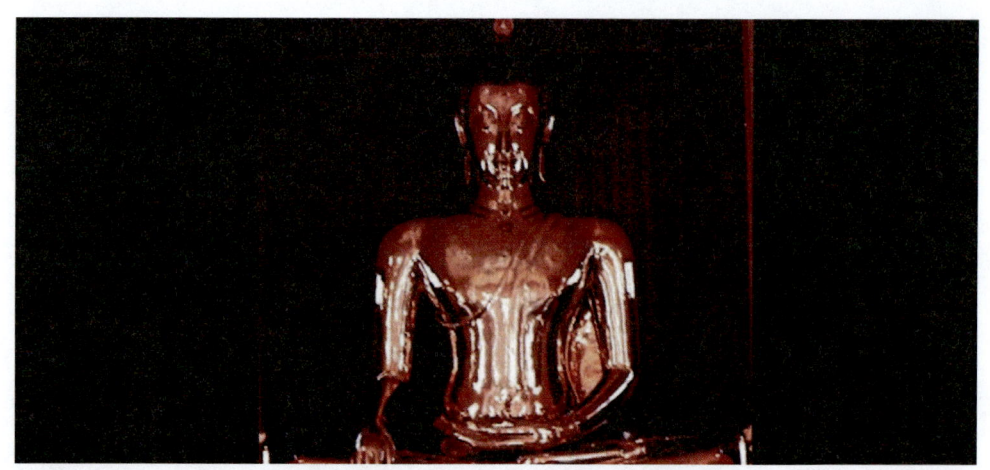

Gold Buddha in East Temple

Temple in Bangkok

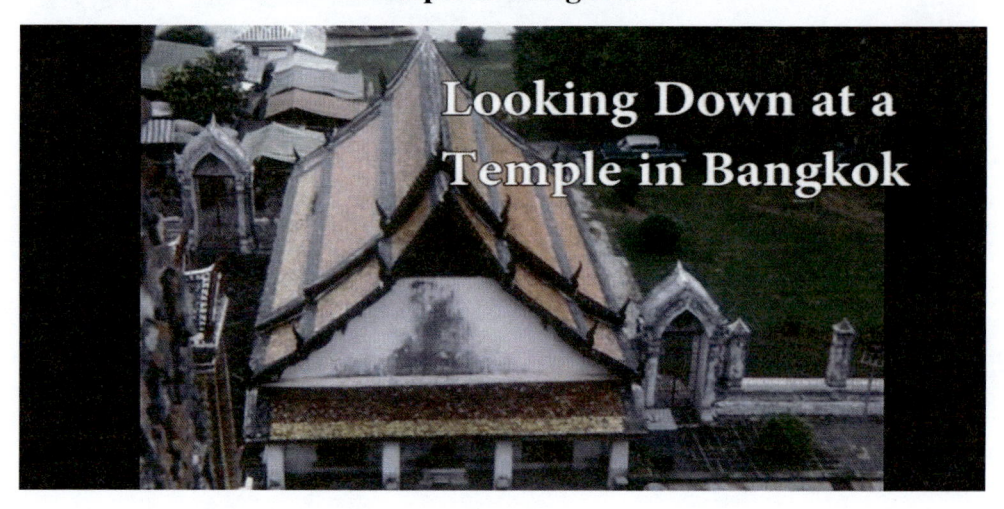

Looking Down at a Temple in Bangkok

Sunrise in Viet Nam 1967

Marble Mountain

Little Bit of Rock and Roll

Sharing Rations With Kids

Route 1 Ho Chi Mon Trail

Bangkok 1967

Bangkok College

Bangkok Temple

Beautiful Girl Dancing

Sunset in Viet Nam 1967

Irrigation of Rice Paddy

Buddhist Temple 1967

Base Camp Viet Nam

Sword Fight in Bangkok

Bangkok Temple

Shopping in Bangkok

Looking Down at a Temple in Bangkok

Bangkok Temple

Downtown Da Nang Vietnam

Funeral Service
In Vietnam, they bury their deceased in circles so the devil can't hide in the corners

One of Many Buddhist Temples

Chapter Four
The Shot Heard Round the City

Now back home my roller coaster life continued.

Shortly after my discharge from the Marines, my girlfriend informed me that she was pregnant. There was no doubt as to the father, she insisted. (In my life it never just rained; it did however pour frequently.) Given my eminent paternity status, a decision had to be made. My choices were limited, given the moral climate. My beloved and I professed our love for one another and agreed to tie the knot. That day stands out in my mind for an intense reason. It was the first time in my entire life anyone had ever told me they loved me.

Later this moment would be looked upon with irony. For some readers I realize that this profession of love that so moved me may come across as minor and unimportant, even routine. For me it was the moral equivalent of winning the lottery. Given what followed… I should have demanded that my beloved take a lie detector test.

At the time she seemed to be the perfect fit – long and blonde. She was blonde, statuesque, sexy and beautiful. She also claimed to be innocent and virginal. The future brought us two children, a girl and a boy. My job as a truck driver for a frozen food company appeared both promising and secure. (Day to day security can produce such myopia, especially spiritually.) We bought a house in Pittsburgh's Sheraden section. It seemed that the 'American Dream' could still come true.

I also purchased the largest insurance policy I could afford. It had a double indemnity clause where if I died via accident, the payment was doubled. Take note of this.

My challenges were far from over. Near our house was a vacant lot, which was a haven for rats. I caught and killed an increasing number of these vermin trying to compete for the babies' cribs. When I confronted the property owner about the situation, he readily understood, he claimed. He "heard our pain' and would do something immediately to correct the situation. I was to learn that the property owner's definition of 'immediately' was significantly different from Webster's. Nothing got done. It was time for radical action. I saved a large bag of dead rats — the ones that he implied didn't exist. I took them to his office in broad daylight and dumped them on his immaculate, important-looking desk.

Speaking of rats, I later learned that my betrothed was having an affair with the guy next door, my best friend, and attempted to seduce my brother. This is not a character assassination; just the unfortunate truth.

Then the next unwelcome adrenaline rush roared into my life. The truck I was driving failed to negotiate a curve on a steep icy mountain road and skidded off a high embankment. The vehicle I was driving was a freezer truck, which is much heaver and somewhat clumsier than other delivery type vehicles. I will remember that day forever: December 17, 1977. I was on Route 30 on Jennerstown Mountain, Pennsylvania. Readers who are familiar with the area will instantly grasp the danger of the situation. That road is treacherous in the summer, let alone on a snowy winter day.

The truck had bald tires and was overloaded. Fortunately, I had the presence of mind to turn off the ignition before the crash, thus averting a Hollywood -style explosion. Before the medics arrived, I did regain consciousness only to find myself hanging from the open door of the cab. It was a long way down.

My freezer truck was carrying frozen turkeys for the holidays, many of which spilled onto the roadside and were ripe for the taking. People were grabbing turkeys and running. I hollered for help but the free turkeys took priority. The ambulance crew, police and firefighters eventually freed me. Later, in the cold light of day, I surveyed the wreckage of my truck and wondered how anyone could have survived. That perennial Higher Power had guided me and protected me once again. And I hadn't even so much as sent Him a thank you card.

I recuperated from the truck accident and collected workmen's compensation. Healing can be a very slow process and I was gaining additional experience. My injuries from that particular brush with the grim reaper put a crimp in my lifestyle. In short order my marital relationship with my wife was zilch, though not due to any lack of desire on my part. I was to discover that wife number one did not subscribe to the time-honored adage "grin and bear it" or "time and love heals all." Soon I had to confront the fact I was competing with other men on what could not be considered a level playing field.

What happened next could have been a plot device in any sleazy soap opera. I confronted my wife about her infidelities. Her response was indifferent, uncaring, but not remorseful. Enough was enough, I decided. This was a marriage in name only; even the concept of family was becoming wobbly. To describe the situation as being on thin ice would be generous. What we had was a cruel circus.

I packed my bags and prepared to leave. My wife protested my exit and played the victim. My bags were in hand and I was reaching for the doorknob. Something spun me around, and with a jolt, I was unconscious. I never saw the muzzle flash of the gun that shot me in the right eye. I don't even remember falling to the floor. However if greed has a smell like a hefty insurance policy with a double indemnity clause, I would have noticed the stench immediately. Much later I awoke from my coma. I attempted to piece the situation together. This puzzle should have had a warning label that read: 'Dangerous and Insane Situation, Proceed With Caution.' My coma was the result of a gunshot wound to my right eye. The slug blinded me in that eye and kept going into my brain. Given the point of impact, I should be D-E-A-D. Fortunately, God saw things very differently.

The police reports never identified my assailant. I have personally ruled out St Frances of Assisi and TV's Mr. Rogers. The assailant(s)/conspirator(s) I suspect were no doubt frustrated beyond words to learn that my life insurance policy remained maddeningly out of reach and intact throughout my coma.

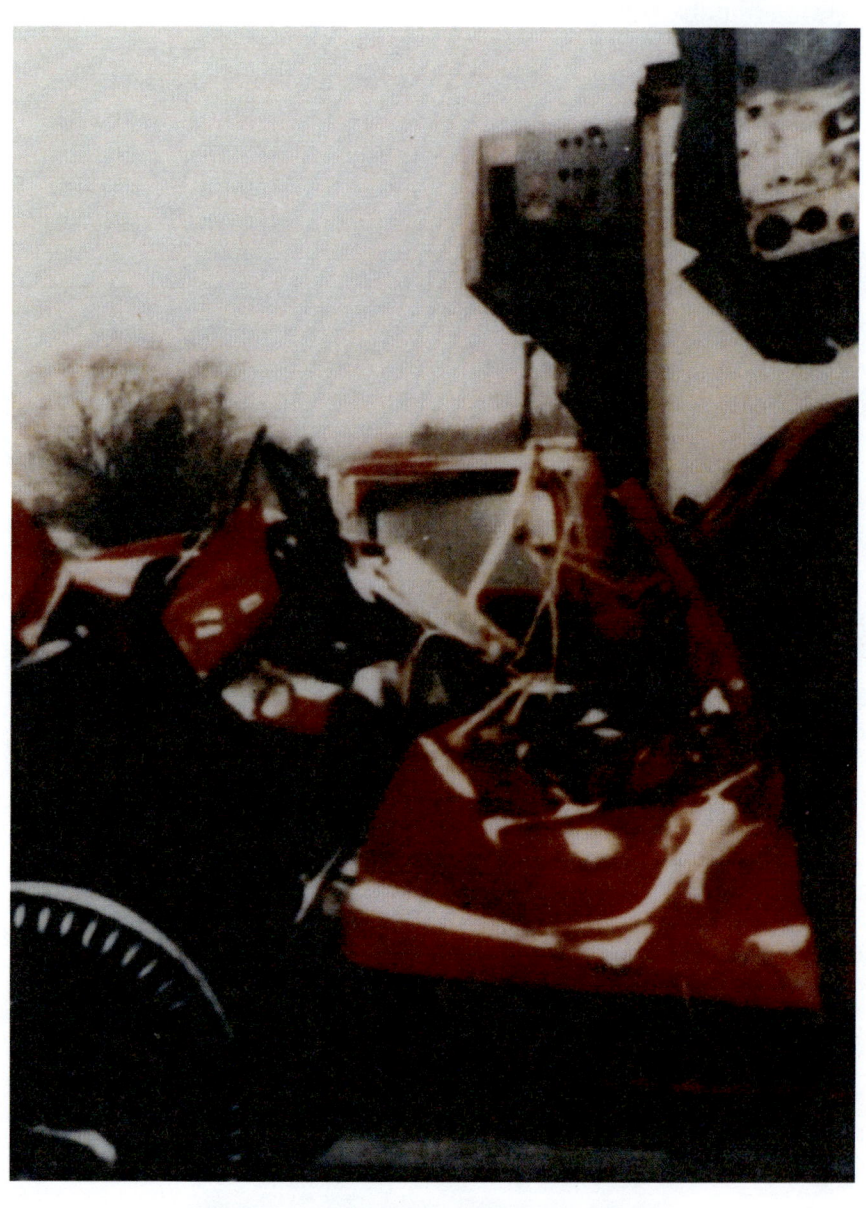

JENNERSTOWN MOUNTAIN, PA
Bald Tires and Overloaded Truck
Driver, Jim Crosson - Dec. 7, 1977

JENNERSTOWN MOUNTAIN, PA
Bald Tires and Overloaded Truck
Driver, Jim Crosson - Dec. 7, 1977

Slowly, at almost glacier speed, full consciousness returned. With generous help from God's Divine Hand, I had defied my well-meaning "friends" who had reasoned the obvious and pronounced me gone. But full consciousness unveiled as many challenges as solutions. It brought with it many questions— searching and pained questions. Overwhelming despair overcame me. Despair is one of Satan's most dependable emissaries; I know this from hard experiences. Frustration erupted within me. I had the perfect excuse to give up. I was tough, but there are limits, no matter who you are. I had definitely reached that limit.

I called out to a God I knew only casually and kept at arms length, hoping He wasn't keeping score. My desperation was matched only by my sincerity. The unspoken question: "Am I going to make it?" screamed from the depths of my soul. I felt lost in a void where no one could hear my cries — or at least ignored them. I was being sucked into a savage, indifferent void. Yet in this dark, seemingly endless space of panic nearing hopelessness, someone did hear my cry. It was answered briefly yet poignantly in the space of one small word — three letters: Y-E-S!

This did not come as a vague whisper but as a word on a blazing, well-lit marquee ... a marquee that was heralding a world premiere event. It was powerful and uplifting in a way that is difficult to describe, yet I knew that not even the darkest skies could dim its light. It was a message at the most crucial time. It was an experience that saved my life.

I did not know Him personally. He heard the cry of this broken sinner, and He reached down into my deep pit of deceit, death and despair and pulled me up. He showed me that no hole is so deep that He isn't deeper still. He washed away my sins and made me a brand new man.

Dark humor and disaster are natural bed partners. When I was in my coma and apparently slipping slowly and inexorably into the great beyond, my sister Candy was at

DEPARTMENT OF POLICE
OFFENSE/INCIDENT REPORT
Page 1
FORM NO. 10
REVISED 1/1/75

OFFENSE: X Accidental Shooting
2. U.C.R. CLASS: 11
3. DISTRICT: 8
4. C.C.R. NO.: 277183
LOCATION OF OCCURRENCE: 813 Dubois St.
APT. NO.: —
TYPE OF PREMISES: Residence
GRID: 2006
DATE AND TIME OCCURRED: 12/21/79 - 1013
DATE AND TIME REPORTED: 12/21/79 - 1013
VICTIM'S NAME: James Crosson
AGE: 32 **SEX:** M **RACE:** W **MARITAL:** M
OCCUPATION: None At Present
VICTIM'S ADDRESS: Same As Location
HOME PHONE: 771-7718
PLACE OF EMPLOYMENT OR SCHOOL: None
VICTIM'S CONDITION: —
VICTIM INJURED ☐ HOSPITAL ☐ DOCTOR ☐ NATURE OF INJURIES
DECEASED ☐

PERSON REPORTING (IF OTHER THAN VICTIM): Wife - Crosson - Same Address
WEAPON/TOOL USED: 6.35 Mauser - Ser# 289930 - Blue Nickel - Brown Wooden Handle
POINT OF ENTRY: Right Eye

NARRATIVE: Mrs. ████ Crosson victims wife stated to us (8,12) that while unloading dishwasher in the kitchen she heard a gunshot in the living room, running into the room wife noticed her husband sitting on the couch with his head slumped down onto the pillow of the couch.
Wife noticed husbands weapon (mentioned Blk #21) laying at his feet on the floor. She picked up the pistol and placed it onto the coffee table at other side of the room. — 852 crew arrived shortly after Medic 3 and assisted them carrying victim to ambulance. — 8K arrived and removed clip from pistol.

REPORTING OFFICERS/BADGE NUMBERS: Joseph Sieber #804 - James Anderson #232
STA.: 8 **VEH. OR POST:** 852
ASSISTING OFFICERS: 8L, 8I
INVESTIGATIONS BR. NOTIFIED: D-12 - DeShantz/Wolfe
STATUS: ☐ Cleared By Arrest ☐ Exceptionally Cleared ☐ Not Cleared ☐ Unfounded
SERGEANT: C Bruno A/O

PITTSBURGH BUREAU OF POLICE
REPORT

VICTIM	DATE/TIME THIS REPORT	DISTRICT	ORIG. C.C.R. NO.
James Crosson	12/21/79 - 1143	8	277183

- Medic 3 told us the gunshot wound was in the eye and at present were unable to disclose condition of the victim.
- 18L notified Homicide and Det. Serafini told him a car will be dispatched as soon as possible.
- Before D-12 arrived - (Det Deshantz + Wolfe) at 1150 hrs, to interrogate the wife about the shooting. We asked Mrs. Crosson how the shooting happened. Mrs. Crosson stated to us that her husband usually cleaned his weapons in the Living room and would place all his guns on the couch, then get the cleaning kit out.
- We could not find empty shell casing and the cleaning kit was still on shelf down the cellar.
- Mrs. Crosson also stated that a shotgun was in the living room fully encased, and she placed it back in the cellar on top of the washing machine after she called the Police. She did this to get the gun out of the room, as she was in a shocked condition.

- 5 Bullets were in pistols clip Make S&W .25 caliber.

C. Bruno #/8
Lieut Nalander

my bedside sobbing uncontrollably over her nearly dead brother. I unexpectedly let go a whopping sneeze, nearly scaring her to death. My shooting was listed as accidental by the Pittsburgh Police, a copy of whose report is included elsewhere in this manuscript. I guess it was easier to write accidental shooting on the report than to actually investigate the incident. Never mind that my gun case was still on the shelf where I kept it.

Never mind that after the plastic bags were taken from my hands at the hospital, no powder burns were found. Powder burns are found in almost all cases of self inflected or close range shootings, accidental or not. My hands had none. My sister Candy made it her business to ask about this detail. The response was negative, no powder burns. The gun that supposedly 'discharged while I was cleaning it' was a twenty-five caliber semiautomatic. A semi-automatic weapon would have expended a shell casing even after only one firing. NO SHELL CASINGS WERE FOUND. To the best of my knowledge, the bullet that resides in my head to this day is most probably a twenty-two caliber. (My wife's boyfriend had that exact weapon.)

For my part, I give the Pittsburgh Police credit for having sirens on their cars, nothing more. While I lay in the hospital hovering between life and death, I became estranged from my children, courtesy of my first wife. She cost me irreplaceable growing up time with them, something I would very much like to discuss with her — face to face.

The gun that I was supposedly shot with was a .25 caliber automatic. Like every automatic, when it fires, it rejects an empty shell. The police never found any such shells. The police, upon arriving at the scene, place plastic gloves on my hands, to preserve any gunpowder residue. When the gloves were taken off at the hospital, no residue was found. Imagine that.

The insurance company would not pay the double indemnity on the $40,000 insurance policy. Instead, my spouse accepted a settlement of $12,000, in exchange for a release, that she convinced me to sign, for our children. Neither me, nor my children, ever saw a dime of it. Comas can be odd. In TV and the movies, comas have the patient as completely out of touch with their surroundings. None of the five senses are working. While I lay in the hospital bed with my head wrapped in bandages I discovered that I could hear but could not respond. I heard my wife's voice along with another. They were not there to console me. The voice I believe was her current boyfriend, the one who I believe shot me. My ex-wife's sentiments were decidedly insensitive. "Let the blankety blank —— die!" she snapped coldly. She had grown fond of the aroma of my life insurance policy with the double indemnity clause.

It was time for a real spiritual education. I was to learn that God was going to take this street kid with a failing grade in faith to the head of the class. My spiritual education was to be full of surprises. If I expected a rose garden to appear before me, I was in for a disappointment. God had extended a long term protective hand on my sorry posterior but there would be still tough times ahead.

Despite all the proof that I had that my shooting was a cold and calculated act, I had to come to the reality that, with me in my debilitated condition, my children had only one person that they could look to for support; and that was their mother. The only reason I didn't have her arrested for attempted murder was because of my fierce love of my children. I didn't want them to end up in a foster home. I had to put aside all anger and feelings or retribution, and push the matter of my wife's guilt, for the sake of the children. I kept on thinking about how Jesus could forgive those people who nailed his hands and feet to the cross, and a new spirit of forgiveness overcame me, and turned me into a new creation.

This time there was a crucial difference; this time problems could be faced with a positive spiritual attitude. Expecting a rose garden is a troublesome pitfall that ensnares many new and backsliding Christians. It is a misleading tendency to assume that the acceptance of Christ means automatically smooth sailing! What it really means is that when the seas of life are at their most stormy, we have a Higher Power that will provide the strength and direction to get us successfully through the most discouraging situation.

My spiritual growth was not to be a simple or an easy affair. My first serious test of faith came as I spent months in depressing VA hospitals. My body healed with maddening slowness. I knew it would never be the same.

This recovery period put me through one of my most severe tests. There are challenges that cause nail biting. Then there are discouragements that push one's sanity to the edge. I was at that point, no two ways about it. If there was a consolation to be had, it was that I WAS NOT ALONE. It is amazing how God, like only He can do, would turn my darkness into the brightest of light.

A multitude of patients that shared my surroundings were in varying stages of either frustration or depression. I saw my fellow sufferers and was determined to help them heal. It would be no small task. I encouraged my fellow veterans to be strong. The quicksand of defeat was all around us, waiting to suck us under. I tried to build bridges to leap the pervasive quicksand. It was a powerful spiritual experience. I saw some vets gain spiritual confidence! Not everybody realized what kind of healing was happening; I hardly understood myself. I've found that spiritual miracles do not always come neatly labeled, but that does not make the miracles any less meaningful.

Scores of overworked, underpaid professionals helped us recover. At times it was like a zoo – madness everywhere. Unless one has been there, it is tough to describe this crowded, noisy, environment filled to the brim with what could easily be dismissed as hopeless cases. Without a dedicated and hardworking staff, all of us would be merely walking through a meaningless healing process — a state of the art treadmill with a beautiful prize just out of reach.

It is important for me to highlight the tireless and dedicated efforts of at least a few staff persons at the VA hospital. Without them, who knows what might have happened to me physically?

Too often these overworked professionals are reduced to pronouns, name tags, anonymous pictures, or forgotten shadows. Even in these absurdly unfavorable environments, God works through people like those rehab workers, performing unheralded miracles daily. Unfortunately, there were some staffers who only waited for his/her paycheck and quitting time. They made the process more difficult than it needed to be.

At one point I tried to start doing things on my own. Along the hallway was a railing that patients used to pull themselves along in their wheelchair. I had to go to the bathroom so I thought I would do this myself. I was tired of asking for help. Getting along the railing was fine but once in the bathroom, I misjudged the safety railings, spun completely around them and wound up lying under the toilet looking up. I have had many low points in my life but that stands out as a low, low, point. I have had to look at ugly and threatening things, but there is something truly discouraging about being on floor, paralyzed, and looking at the bottom of a toilet. God gave me the strength to pull myself back into my wheelchair so I could return to my room.

I shared my room with a man named Evan. He was lying in bed; he had both of his legs gone and was not wearing his prosthetics. I wheeled into the room looking for a glass of water from our bed stand. I reached for the glass, overextended myself and tipped the wheelchair. I fell onto the floor, knocked over the glass of water and made enough noise to wake Evan. He went to get up from his bed, but forgot that he had no legs. He fell right on top of me. We looked like two fish out of water. The nurse walked in and asked " Are you from 'chaos-is-us' or what? "

For me, two people, a nurse and a therapist, were special but I mean no disrespect to all the others. The nurse I dubbed the 'Dragon Lady'. The therapist, Penny, I named 'Thunder Lizard'. They were two extremely dedicated people.

Let's talk about the nurse. Under her hard as nails professional persona this tenacious savior had an enormous heart. She also had a name: Bert Davis. Her title was Head Nurse. When my arm was paralyzed, it was the Dragon Lady who challenged me to several bouts of arm wrestling. She did this on an inconvenient day. I had a pity party scheduled for myself. I wanted to go to bed (it was 5:00 PM!). She had other plans for me. "You can go to bed if you arm wrestle me." I could not refuse. A casual onlooker might have seen a rough and tumble game of arm wrestling going on between patient and nurse. I'm sure it looked nothing like therapy. And that was the way it seemed to me at first. What was really going on was a tough love miracle. Bert was determined that I gain control of my arm. She did not give up easily. Once, from sheer frustration, I kicked Ms. Davis under the table. It should put an end to her annoying demands. I was wrong. She kicked me back. Arm wrestling continued each day and so did my recovery.

Let's talk about Penny. She was officially a Physical Therapist. She too, thank God, demanded more of my recovering body than I thought I could give. She would come into my room and say "We are going for a walk today." My reply was "I can't. I can't." By the third 'I can't', we were already walking. She did not accept 'no' for an answer. Neither lady was on the Six o'clock News, but they performed miracles nonetheless.

While the Dragon Lady and her associates taught me to walk again, spiritual miracles were occurring. These nurses lifted me emotionally when I threatened to throw in the towel. The only towel they were willing to permit being 'thrown in' was the one with the sweat off my brow after a workout. These women were pushy and persistent; we need more like them. I understand Bert Davis has been called home to the great Rehab Center in the sky.

I made progress, slow but measurable. Lots of minor successes became major milestones. I thought this stay in the hospital was the ultimate test… but that was yet to come.

Chapter Five
"Getting Serious About God"

While I lay in the VA hospital in Pittsburgh I became estranged from my son and my daughter, courtesy of my first wife. Even when I was coming out of the coma, she stubbornly kept them away. I have been told by dependable sources that my kids were told I was dead. Wife number one cost me irreplaceable growing up time with them, something I would very much like to discuss with her—face to face. I realize that my demand is as unrealistic.

I knew my body would never be the same. Physically athletic, active Jim Crosson was no more. I would always be feisty and sharp of wit but I could only count on limited cooperation from my body. This recovery period put me through one of my most severe tests. I was to go through overwhelming bouts of depression and anxiety. Some challenges induce nail biting. Then there are challenges that push one's sanity to the edge. I was at that point.

I became a "recluse" of sorts. My personal recollection is hazy but the Physical Therapist told me that there were days when I didn't even attempt to get out of bed. I couldn't even picture my body whole again or even functioning. I was surrounded by people in uniform making me do things I had no interest in doing. Those were dark days indeed, in sharp contrast to what would come later. But, I was too wrapped up in my own personal cataclysm to care about reaching out.

Without spiritual help, the bouts of depression were enough to end me. I'm sure God saw this and sent veteran order. As I spoke of earlier, the gunshot to my eye not only ended my eyesight, it sparked epileptic seizures that were both major and terrifying at first.

It was unmistakably time for a custom tailored stress test for one James Francis Crosson. But now there was a momentous difference. While there would still be tough times, problems could be faced with a positive attitude and a constructive spiritual strength. I was not alone, although I felt that way for many days. A multitude of patients, in varying degrees of frustration or depression, shared my surroundings. All of us were in trying circumstances. Day in and day out, I saw my fellow sufferers. I had no idea that eventually I would be helping those who were in as sad a shape or worse than I was in.

I received psychological testing and evaluation out the wazoo. Throughout the medical reports can be seen the phrases "accidentally shot himself" and other charming variations. One such written report, done in July of 1980 describes me as "severely depressed [due to marital separation and loss of contact with his children] and, in a classic of understatement, "not knowing what the future holds for him."

Other glorious insights that appear on that same July of 1980 report include that "He shows denial of his illness... [and] does not acknowledge that his blindness is anything more than mildly incapacitating and talks as though he can make a substantial recovery in the future." The section that followed was a real hoot, given what I'm sure really happened. I was described as a "suspicious individual [who] does not trust most others, even those... close to him."

My evaluator did find some optimism He wrote: "In light of the role of his depression [resulting from] his current marital difficulties, and his desire to protect his privilege to see his children, his wife should be contacted in order to have her intentions clarified." If that last line were part of a stand-up routine in a nightclub, the audience would be in the aisles. If I needed to have my wife's intentions clarified any further, I should be equipped with a bulletproof vest and respectable defensive firepower.

I was evaluated for suicidal tendencies, as were all veterans. They decided I had none. On this point they were dead accurate, no pun intended. I have never been a candidate for the Early Bus to the Promised Land, no matter how difficult my life got.

My evaluation reminded me of an incident that occurred in Vietnam. A close friend in Nam took his own life by a bullet to his head. According to my interview records, reporting accurately this time, I am quoted as saying of my friend's suicide: "He died in my arms... [blood and body parts] were all over my jacket. I don't know how anyone can do that. You just have to pick yourself up and keep going, no matter what happens." I remember that incident well. The soldier, one of the few servicemen in our unit who was not a Marine, had simply reached the end of his rope. In Vietnam that was a very real possibility. I begged him to get a grip and to calm down, to no avail.

The whole episode was over with alarming speed. He did a panicky monologue that was incoherent except to him— then the gun went to his head. The point of no return came a second later.

My medical report continues: "This [persistently positive attitude] seems to be Jim's philosophy, and it should help him succeed with further rehabilitation." I had another in an endless series of psychological evaluations. Highlights of this session are included because it was one of the more responsible and productive sessions the VA provided for me. It reads: "Veteran is interested in vocational counseling and states he wants to do something productive with his life. We have agreed to begin with an interest inventory to begin to clarify a vocational direction. Of utmost importance is the nature of Mr. Crosson's disabilities and setting realistic goals for him to achieve."

My actual work history, colorful and checkered though it was, may or may not have been useful to these people. I had been a warehouse foreman, a job I not only performed well but also enjoyed; a chipper/welder in a mill a security guard, a 'migrant worker' and a magazine salesman.

I progressed, at first by inches. In the early days of my rehabilitation, I was, I am told, a model of non-cooperation. This was a good sign because most serious injury patients go into a shell at first. This is not uncommon among severe head trauma patients.

I finally accepted my situation.

It was a mighty spiritual experience played out against a background that did not always lend itself to hope. I watched fellow vets who might have given up hope, this time gain spiritual confidence. Few, I think, realized that a spiritual healing was taking place. I hardly understood myself. Miracles do not come neatly labeled.

Then I reached out. God wanted me to help others. I didn't feel so sad for myself anymore.

I think the first veteran I actually helped to recover was a guy who had been confined to bed for an extended time —heart attack victim as I recall. I believe he was nearly bored to death. The street boy Jimmy Crosson played doctor, this time with good results. We started talking and I convinced him to sit up. Shortly, he was on his feet. (I can picture readers aghast in horror at this nut, playing doctor with a heart attack victim. Give me a moment before you decide.) He reached for his 'Cadillac,' a wheelchair. I had my own pet names for virtually everything in the VA hospital.

I dissuaded him from using his wheelchair, figuring he had been 'welded' to mechanical supports for too long. Using me as support, the veteran and I walked down the hallway. He seemed surprised that he could walk at all.

He was even more surprised that there was still a world beyond his bed. Part way through our walk he asked about his wheelchair. "Should we use it?" The Marine Corps mind-set re-surfaced in me. Playfully I chanted "There's no need in turning back, you just lost your Cadillac". We went down to a basement courtyard. My newly found friend was happily amazed. He marveled aloud. Once again I quipped: "Welcome to the future, man, it's already in progress."

I had a lot of fun with senior citizen patients at the VA. I used to walk into their ward and announce, "Alright you guys, let's get those pacemakers synchronized." They smiled and moved around a little. I kidded with them knowing that nothing is better for recovery than a positive mental attitude, a key part of which is a sense of humor.

I made sure that respect was a part of any game we played. I wanted to emphasize that I laughed with them not at them. Frequently in conversations, my military service would come up. I told them I served in the Big One. Their eyes would go wide. "One so young", they marveled, "actually serving in the Big One? Did you serve in WWI or II?" "Neither," I would respond with straight face. "I served in Vietnam." My stock would take a bit of a slide. But I always came back and always got them going. This humor and positive mental attitude would prove itself to be a lifesaver in days to come.

Once, Penny woke me and told me we were going for a walk. It would be therapeutic ...it would help me to get better. My stock response was an irritated and agonized, "I'm paralyzed! I can't walk! Go away! " She nodded that she understood, but she persisted in this irrational goal. The third time my protest left my mouth, it was admittedly less respectful. But this third time, I made a discovery. I had left my bed, taken half a dozen "impossible" steps and was part way across the room!!!

Physical therapy involved exercises and activities that most people take for granted. Bending. Standing. Walking. Frequently after brain or head trauma, the "central switchboard" is down and communications have to be reestablished with the land below the neck. Physical fitness enthusiasts encourage us to listen to our bodies for signals of progress or damage. I had to do much the same thing—get acquainted with my body again.

Standing was achievable. Walking was another story. First it was for short distances — just a very few feet. Then, patiently and carefully, a few feet further; using braces and other mechanical helpers. I was told that this would be a painstaking process. For me the word that best described it was eternal. Patience was never a virtue with me.

I was reliving infancy. First baby steps, then standing on my own and then more physical therapy. I spent considerable time not only in Physical Therapy but also in Occupational Therapy. OT teaches you how to cook again, how to do chores and how to live on your own again. Endless exercising made the clock move ahead for me as my body was reacquainted with my brain.

In sharp contrast to the eulogies that had been prematurely written for me, I put new, humorous names on things I experienced. For example, I dubbed Physical Therapy "Physical Terrorism."

Today I am told that many of the 'pressure' methods that worked so well on myself and others are now illegal because they are to the "detriment" of the patient. I can't help but think the laws are written by those who have never worked in a Rehab Center. They do not have a practical concept of what hands on rehabilitation is all about.

I felt the Lord's powerful hand in my life; my attitude did a complete turnaround. My previous vision of the word YES left an indelible impression. I knew that no tribulation could stand in my way. That guy on the cross had changed all that. I saw my fellow sufferers in a different light. This time I reached out to them with purpose. I was determined to help them heal. It would be no small task. I knew that it was the intervention of the Lord in my life that made the task possible at all.

I encouraged my fellow veterans to be strong. I had a special sense of bonding with those who were hurting as I had. They too would face a detailed, painstaking, step-by-step process wherein a patient goes from being a potential vegetable to a functioning human being. It is important to me to highlight Bert Davis and Penny and the others whom I cannot remember. Without them, who knows what might have happened to me, physically and spiritually? Too often these overworked professionals are reduced to pronouns, name tags, or forgotten altogether. Even under these absurdly unfavorable circumstances, God works through people like those rehab workers, performing unheralded miracles daily.

At one point I tried doing things on my own in the Veterans Hospital. I got tired of being told, "We'll get to you when we get to you," by less motivated staff persons. Along the hallways was a railing that wheelchair bound patients could pull themselves along. On one occasion I had to go to the bathroom so I decided now was a good time to do this myself. After all, eventually I would be doing this on my own. Getting along the railing went well enough but once in the bathroom, I guess I misjudged the safety railings, spun completely around them and wound up lying flat on the floor under the toilet looking up. I have had many low points in my life but that stands out as a classic low point. In my life I have had to look at many unpleasant sights, some of them square in the eye. But there is something truly discouraging about laying paralyzed on the floor of a bathroom looking at the bottom of a toilet that is memorable for all the wrong reasons.

For every depressing, frustrating episode in the VA hospital there was one that was riotously laughable. Still determined to conquer this bathroom business on my own, I got myself back to my wheelchair and rode it back to my room. I shared a room with a guy named Evan, a wonderful person of whom I have since lost track.

Evan had lost both his legs to disease and was just getting used to artificial limbs. On this day, he was fast asleep.

Once in the room, I reached for a glass of water on the night stand. This should have been a minor task, but, I missed the glass and it fell to the floor with a loud thud. I also fell with my own thud. Evan awoke with a start, sat upright, forgot he didn't have his legs on, swung out of bed and landed on top of me. It was bedlam, but it was beautiful bedlam. We looked like two fish out of water, flailing around. A nurse glanced in at this confusion. Without skipping a beat, she asked dryly, "Where are you guys from-chaos is us?" She then proceeded to put us back in order.

I made slow but measurable progress. Eventually I became much more cooperative with Penny and others. I even earned to use my braces and walk during physical therapy. I am proud of the fact that soon nurses would go by my room and find me doing my prescribed exercises.

My mind was finally set on getting better. The calendar slowly became my friend. Minor successes become milestones.

Penny's persistently positive attitude overcame my most dogged resistance. She told me recently that she loves her job and particularly loves seeing people get better. With Penny, it is more than just a paycheck. It is, as with Bert Davis the Dragon Lady, a life's mission. I was told that Bert was far more interested in seeing others heal than taking care of herself. I wish her a long life. When I was ready to leave, she came to my bedside and growled "you look here, fool, you go there, keep working hard, and I want to see you when you get back!"

My next stop was the Massachusetts Center for the Blind in Florence, Massachusetts. It was July 7, 1980 when I began my stay. After that, I ended up in the VA Medical Center in Northhampton, Massachusetts. I became part of Northhampton Blind Rehabilitation Program. The following month I was transferred to the West Haven Low Vision Clinic where I stayed two weeks. With such a diverse medical background, I should have simply hung around, got a degree, and became a doctor. I'm told that my medical files were getting as thick as Webster's Unabridged Dictionary. Throughout these records was the annoyingly repetitive "accidental shooting". Fortunately to offset this, another phrase is repeated: "veteran is anxious to get on with his life and do something productive".

I returned to Northampton and called it home for several months. Like the Oakland Veterans hospital, it required me to reach deeply into myself for the resources to heal. I continued to help other veterans. They were enhancing my spiritual growth.

Several hours of therapy were received every day. I will proudly add here that the staff did not have to force therapy on me. I went to P. T. willfully. It became second nature. I had a motivation they knew nothing about. I knew what would happen if Ms. Dragon Lady or Penny discovered that I had been lazy. That was not a pleasant thought.

Another therapeutic exercise that caught my attention was swimming. Three times a week at the Center for the Blind, I was in the water, making my best attempt to give existing waterfowl a run for their money. On this point my keepers and I were on the same page. Two progress reports with my name on them dated July and December of 1982 give me high marks: "This patient attends therapeutic swimming three times weekly. We will continue with his present program in an effort to have the patient relax while swimming to help increase motion. [Mr. Crosson] states that he likes the therapeutic swim program [since] it makes him feel stronger and helps him relax." The water makes the body more buoyant and thus makes movement easier.

They apparently also helped control my seizures with Dilantin. I fought a truly uphill battle with depression. My wife was out of the picture but so were my kids. One was as unimportant as the other was important.

I moved on to Occupational Therapy, that is teaching one to do for oneself. They also do a lot of work with alcohol abuse patients. I am legally blind but my trainers ruled out teaching me Braille. I was told that the brain would reject Braille if any measurable amount of eyesight exists. At the Center for the Blind, I worked with a therapist that was marvelous. His name was Gene Sloan. His official title was "mobility instructor". It was his job to see that patients were truly "up and at 'cm". He would take patients out in the car, park it and have them walk for varying distances before coming back to the car. As part of this "mobility training" I earned to listen for cars more than the average person. This has been very useful since I have no peripheral vision on the right side.

Behind the Center was a Bowling Alley that was frequented by my fellow patients. I'll admit I am not a bowler but it was nonetheless disconcerting to have totally blind people beat me at bowling. I countered my losses at bowling by arguing, in jest, that they should let me bowl overhand.

Anyone who has dealt with alcoholics and their rehabilitation will tell you that it is a challenge to say the least. Substance abusers, be they of drug or alcohol, have mastered the art of denial, even when they wind up in rehab. I remember one comic experience in the washroom at the

Center. I think I was cleaning my teeth and had a brand new bottle of Scope on the counter by the mirror. For we non-alcoholics, the fact that Scope contains nearly 20% alcohol is pretty meaningless. But this apparently meant something to one alcoholic. He barely acknowledged me. He simply grabbed my bottle of Scope and drank it straight down. Any port in a storm, I guess.

It is ironic that for every selfless professional that helped us, there was one staff person who apparently only waited for quitting time. To those people (who I believe are in a minority), I make a simple request: walk a mile in my shoes. Then tell me or other suffering veterans that, "we'll get to you whenever." Dedicated, trained and caring professionals will always ensure success.

During this time, my ex-wife earned a place in a dark corner of anonymity for her role in estranging me from my children, refusing them any contact with me; systematically filling their heads with contempt for me. My daughter and I are estranged but my son Jim Jr. and I get along fine. Her goal, I think, was to turn me into an island overcome by depression. I had been a confirmed sinner, but I don't think I deserved that. A backhanded compliment is in order. She gave her evil purpose one heck of a try. Fortunately, God was tougher.

Very shortly after my release from the Low Vision Center yet another milestone was reached in my life. It was not a pleasant one, but necessary. I came home to find my longtime friend, Ed Wolf, dying of cancer. In his final hours I tried my darnedest to give him whatever 'street boy' Biblical counseling I could muster. I have been through many challenges in my life, some of them truly heartbreaking, but this was among the toughest. Among the Wolf's final words were: "Jim, I don't want to die'. It was an unmistakable plea for help. My sense of powerlessness was overwhelming. I was privileged to pray with him while he awaited his unavoidable final call from the Maker. Ed Wolf's funeral was enormous. Even people who didn't especially like him mourned his passing; one could not stay mad at the Wolf for long.

For me it was the end of an era. Ed Wolf was far from perfect, but I believe the Lord sent him to me when I needed help the most. He was, like the title of that old time movie, an angel with a dirty face. I realize that most of the people who read this work have never met Ed Wolf and obviously never will.

But when we run across those imperfect but impossibly dependable people… who stay with you when common sense dictates they should leave, we have met Ed Wolf. All of us will meet many people throughout the course of our lives. Only a tiny percentage of those will be angels with the name Wolf. Sometimes they will bear another name. Nonetheless, his spirit will be there.

It occurs to me in working to put together this manuscript that this chapter, at least judging by the number of pages in it, is not the largest in the book. Length not withstanding, it is however the most important chapter. Everything leads up to this point. It represents the huge upswing in my life, making up for all the downturns. This is the chapter that I assume will be most beneficial and most uplifting to readers everywhere.

Imagine that if God can give His love and do all this for a sinner such as I, imagine how much more He would do for His other children.

And Looking Toward the Lord, Life Got Better...

Chapter Six
Some Closing Thoughts

I look back and realize that I was called to travel a long and difficult road. Everything has its price; the journey of spiritual growth is not exempt. I cannot regret that because it makes me what I am today. God brought me great healing and purpose in the midst of despair. I realize that there are those readers who would find the whole concept of suffering and hardship unattractive. No matter, we will all suffer at some point...the only question that really matters is how much we are willing to pay to go from ordinary "religious experience" to powerful spiritual growth.

Please hear what I have to say. There is no hole so deep that God isn't deeper still. He has already been there. I seek refuge in the Lord, and if you do the same, God will receive you. He will educate you and show you. Prayer is not a spiritual wish list. Talk to Him about how you feel and He will answer.

On the subject of everything having its price, I would be seriously remiss if I did not add a deeply personal note. My mother survived that hellish day of my confrontation in the attic. She was to pay an enormous price. I realize it could be debated whether or not her subsequent and severe addiction to alcohol and death were directly connected to my stepfather.

This striking blonde woman who could be firm and unyielding to strangers became a slave to my stepfather. I remember watching a truly twisted sense of justice being played out. On the one hand, my stepfather did not hesitate punching my mother in the face, especially if she stood up to him. Then came the kicks to the ribs. His way of "apologizing" was to have her fix her hair and makeup like it was in her professional dancing days and takes her out to the local bar for a fish sandwich.

There are those, I'm sure, who would judge my mother severely for being less strong than she might have been, and for using the bottle as an escape. This however was in the late fifties and times were very different. There were men with holdout attitudes who believed that suffrage was a big mistake. Today I feel a sense of sorrow and guilt that I wasn't more understanding and supportive of her needs or if nothing else, more sensitive to her plight.

When my mother died, she and my stepfather lived in a trailer park in Valley Forge, Pa. From what I've pieced together, the exodus that brought them to that location was less than noble.

She felt trapped in a relationship that she could not escape, at least not safely. The massive cerebral hemorrhage that claimed her life was most likely a blessing. The struggle was over for her.

It would be an understatement to say I have had exposure to life's ups and downs. My ups were rapid and short lived. The downs were generally black and blue. Some people are said to be "cut out" to follow certain callings in life— doctors, lawyers, and mechanics. I realize now that my youthful background qualified me eminently to excel in any number of controversial "careers" such as robber, rapist, junkie, or some combination of the above.

I had the resume for it. Circumstances were perfect to spawn the next deadly serial ... whatever. Chance or coincidence cannot be credited with the fact that I was none of the above. God can take the credit. Only His Love, concern and Power could have protected me and redirected me, not only then but to this day. This I admit is bold talk coming from a street boy who was convinced he could depend on no one but himself— and definitely no one invisible.

Do I regret these experiences? Am I resentful or bitter? I have been told that I have a right to check all of the above. It's true that I would never wish and of these calamities on anyone. I certainly do not wish to repeat them. But for what these experiences have taught me, I do not regret them. These numerous trips down rocky roads have demanded growth of me and created insight that has proven invaluable. I still suffer the aftermath of paralysis and I don't live in a palatial mansion. And I suspect that my infomercial is some ways into the future.

God doesn't always bless people like that. Sometimes the blessings are meaningless by the worlds' measure, but are beyond measurement to those who are blessed. Above all, I rejoice because the Lord has indeed brought healing and purpose to my life in the midst of the most unbearable despair. He has sent people to help along the way. Predictably, since He does work in strange and mysterious ways, my blessings have sometimes come from unexpected and eye opening directions.

I am paralyzed on my left side; by medical standards I should be dead. Remember, I have my own death certificate. But for the extraordinary level of damage my body has suffered, I am without pain throughout my body. I have a bullet in my head, yet I do not suffer headaches. (I tell audiences that I am into heavy metal.) I should be wheelchair bound but I can walk to town. Yes, I have numerous blessings for which to thank Him.

I want to share my recovery and hope, for all those who may need it. Maybe this is especially aimed at those who are convinced they can do it alone. You can't.

There was the person who led me to a dynamic, Bible believing church where I could sense the spirit of God and come to realize the miraculous way that God has permitted me to survive so many hopeless circumstances.

Another blessing is my Christian wife, Lorraine, who now shares my love. This is a true love that secular values cannot possibly hope to fathom, but it is a love that can only come from God.

My wife is fond of cautioning others about what they pray for lest they may get it. She cites an example from her own life. With a wry smile, she will explain that she prayed for patience — and got me!

I tell audiences that I do not know who my dad is but I know who my Father is. I don't want sympathy or pity. Both may be helpful in small doses but both have an enormous capacity for abuse. My purpose both in life and in this work is to share a God who helped me survive and benefit from events that should have destroyed me.

This redemption is not a blessing that can happen only to me. I have no special Divine Redemption. Whatever bedevils you in life can be washed by Him for YOU! I can ...the light at the end of the tunnel -- make that broad statement because I have been to hell and back. Along the way I have sinned and violated enough of the Commandments that God would have a perfect right to slam the door in my face. That brings us to a very important point: No matter who are —no matter how down and out you are... GOD CAN HELP! ... as long as you are willing to turn your life in the direction

He wants you to go. I am living proof that God works with raw, sometimes really raw, material.

God's work goes even a step further than that. No man is an island. My stepfather discovered that the hard way. We need to reach out to one another. We need to be sensitive to the needs of others. The person who may be reading this book, who is convinced there is no hope, needs to be shown His Path. He/she needs to learn that God is in charge and WILL help.

**Lorraine,
the Christian wife who now shares my life...**

Concentration camp survivor and devout Christian Corrie Tenbloom frequently quotes a saying that goes: "There is no pit so deep that He is not deeper still." I agree completely. There's a verse of scripture that reads: "If God be for us, who can be against us?" Stop and think about the powerful message in those ten words. Nothing else in life can offer that kind of hope, at least not dependably and long range.

I ask the reader to forgive me if I preach. It is not my way to bore people with words. In fact it is a real irony that I should be involved in collaborating on a book, since I read very little all during my life. But when such a powerful, valuable solution comes along, it should be shared with everyone.

Life is picture perfect on television and in the movies. Real life is often flawed and unfair. The world that we long for on the screen lasts only as long as that artificial image is before us. Suffering is part of life; it is unavoidable. We all have our crosses to bear.

To some I'm sure that will be a turnoff. This is a world that pretends that "quick fixes" are how problems are solved. That attitude is sad because it misses a crucial point. Because there is a painful side to one's life or a situation, does not mean we have been abandoned or forgotten by the One who matters most. We need not feel abandoned if we identify and accept a Savior who is there to help us and bring us into oneness with Him. Only a fortunate few will not endure pain and suffering in this life… and perhaps they are not especially fortunate. Theirs is more likely a false sense of security. We should expect hard times. The glorious truth is this: NO ONE NEEDS TO STAY DOWN AND OUT AS LONG AS THEY HAVE CHRIST AT THE CENTER OF THEIR LIVES!

This has been a story of God. I am pleased He chose me to star in this draft. My most fervent hope is that it will help many of those, or even one desperate soul, to hang in there and find The Way. Possibly I should have called this a treasure map because that's what it is —a treasure map accompanied by a friendly word of advice: there is powerful spiritual treasure before you. Don't just stand there — DIG.

I realize that this testimony is largely about the past. The past is history. The present is now. Now is a gift. That is probably why they call it the "present". So embrace it; enjoy it and thank God for it, for it is only "now" once.

This is a story of how a victim became victor. It is a story about God and his work in my life. While I walked through the valley, I was truly never alone. This is proof that there is no hole so deep, that he is not deeper still.

**Never Ending Story
Post Script—**

Through my travels in life, I have learned a couple things – the most important is the power of prayer. Another is that to achieve Eternal Life one must receive the Son of God in their lives and form their own personal relationship with Him. I would like to share this knowledge with you in a prayer – I will pray asking God to receive everyone's prayer through my lips. And I when I pray, and you agree with me, please feel free to say 'Amen'. You must remember that life on this earth is a temporary. Eternal life is forever.

Let us pray together: "Dear Lord, we all come before Your throne to give You praise and to give You thanks for the gift of life and to give thanks for Your son Jesus, the greatest gift of all. Jesus… who died on that cross to save us from Satan. Jesus, who we receive as our Lord and Savior… to come and reside within us and fill us with His anointing presence. It is the name of Jesus that we pray loud and proud asking you to forgive us for our sins and shortcomings, cleanse us, grant us redemption, receive us into Your Kingdom, take away all our wicked ways. We truly thank you for our families. Please place them in a hedge of Your protection so that they remain healthy and spiritually safe. O Lord God, we must all submit our life on earth and our physical bodies to death, but today we willingly submit our eternal soul to You. Please guide us and keep us, for we place everything in thy hands, in the name of the Son of God, Jesus Christ, our Lord, our Master, our Redeemer… Amen.

Now, if you have prayed that prayer with me, and you have received Christ in your life, you should rejoice and be glad, for today you are saved and are born again, and you have eternal life.

Be sure to teach everyone you can about God, and how he so much loved you and me, that he let his own Son, Jesus, to be sacrificed on the cross to save us from Satan; and, to those whom God has saved, are saved indeed. Pray, to form you own personal, intimate relationship with God and, as you pray, you will understand the power of prayer. And, the more you pray, the sooner you will learn the truth, and the truth will set you free! Hallelujah!

DEDICATIONS

I dedicate this book to our Heavenly Father, for it is by His grace that I survived and by his love that I am what I am today.

I also want to thank Dan Agona, Mike Pochan and John Fonzo, special people who provided their time and assistance in helping me make this book possible.

I've put 29 years into this book - living, loving and laughing. I look at it this way, one cannot force open the petals of a rose; but, when that time is right, it will open up to you. This testimony is the same, God will open up the opportunity to you, in His time.

To God, be all praise and worship, forever. Amen.

CLOSING THOUGHTS

Let all readers understand that, I don't wish to dwell on the past. It is necessary to recall these events in order to share with you God's blessings, in the extreme. The past is the past, the future is what you make of it, with God's help and in his time.

I've been blessed very handsomely by God and the time has come for me give something back. Which is why I'm in the process of forming this non-profit fund where I will help those are spiritually and financially worthy of saving.

I have been working on this testimony for the last twenty-nine years. Because the time was <u>not just right</u>, I'd not had much success. I look at it this way, you cannot force open the petals of a rose, but when the time is just right it will open up to you. This testimony is the same way. God will use it when the time is just right. So please understand the time <u>is</u> just right! I will be sharing the word of God's works with everyone. And I hope to have the belief and support of my fellow Christians.

PROCEEDS FROM THIS BOOK

Upon receiving these contributions and love offerings I will put them in a non-profit fund. We will make sure God's money gets to those whom God has chosen. This is another random act of Love by God.

I feel it's important that people understand my plans. I plan to complete my calling by starting this non-profit fund of which I have a dear friend who's a corporate lawyer who will assist. I <u>will</u> help those people physically, spiritually, and financially worthy of, along with a card stating: "Just Another Random Act of **Love by God**! With the prayers and the strength of our faith, I will glorify God by serving his children. That is my calling and my plan. With me there is no "Plan B". Remember! This testimony is what it is and is for the glory of <u>Jesus</u>! He is my Lord, <u>God</u>, and Savior, Amen! Your donations and contributions to assist this ministry are welcomed and appreciated.

Kindly send whatever love offering is proper to the name and address below. This <u>will</u> happen.

James Crosson,
611 Chestnut St, Irwin, PA 15642